The Sacred Messenger
A Journey of Spiritual Awakening and Divine Connection

Aliya Griffin

I0110753

Aliya Griffin

The Sacred Messenger
A Journey of Spiritual Awakening and Divine Connection
Copyright © 2025 Aliya Griffin

Aliya Griffin

Dedication

This book is dedicated to my daughter, Mia Loren. Although I mention throughout this book that my spiritual journey is lonely and I have to walk it alone, always in the periphery, rooting me on and my motivation to take step after step, was my little light of love. Miza Piza, my baby girl. I love you. You're literally my reason for living. Thank you for being my support, for believing in me and for keeping me grounded in sanity. I loved you then, now, always and forever.

Aliya Griffin

The Sacred Messenger
A Journey of Spiritual Awakening and Divine Connection

What if a mysterious presence from beyond held the key to your spiritual awakening?

As a psychic, empath, medium/channel, and past life regressionist, I thought I understood the language of spirit—until Noatok appeared. Across five past life regression sessions and an intuitive psychic reading, an extraordinary presence made itself known: an otherworldly and luminous child of Brazilian descent, described in vivid detail by multiple, unconnected clients. His name was Noatok, and his wisdom carried a resonance I couldn't ignore.

At the peak of my own painful spiritual awakening, Noatok emerged as a beacon of guidance and love, reaching across the veil to offer me clarity, healing, and an undeniable connection to something greater. He wasn't just a passing spirit—he was a part of me created from pure love, sent to awaken me to a deeper truth and understanding.

This is my true story of transformation, spirit communication, and the unseen forces that shape our lives in ways we may never fully understand. If you've ever felt the pull of the unknown, sensed a guiding presence, or yearned to unravel the mysteries of your soul's journey, Noatok: The Sacred Messenger will open your heart and mind to the magic waiting just beyond the veil.

Aliya Griffin

Foreword

awakening

it's a fascinating story of life. living. and the struggle to process and embrace her 'higher-self's core-intent and purpose' and the mysterious reoccurrence of a whimsical spirit-child, whose energy vibrated love and grace across echoes of space and time to lift the veil and champion her journey as she navigated through personal doubt and trepidation at the intersectionality between the cavern of her soul's old and new beginnings and spiritual awakening

it's the coming of age of an old. welcomed familiar whose signs and symptoms of its coming to pass was engraved in the stars eons before she was even a twinkle in her father's eye it's a spiritually hereditary. genetically engineered silver-cord connection to our spirit-family's soul-line ...a gravitational pull. bottled and capped and forged in the baptism of fire and discernment with the full power of all the spiritual ancestors

this divine calling has shadowed her always. giving voice to its persistent and audible urgings as she tiptoed around the sleeping beauty of its phenomime – i.e., her considerable attributes. gifts. and genuine psychic abilities that played through her life like a movie. her natural inclination towards all things spiritual. and her connection to the spirit-world. her affinity with spirits. spiritual discourse. tarot cards. her gift for helping people root-out and heal inter-generational soul-trauma and psychic-wounds ...it's a calling that cannot be denied once its season has arrived – and it has now arrived!

it's a gentle reminder that you can run but you cannot hide from what's meant for you. and that 'nothing' is impossible if you know who you are and have faith enough to step into your fear and embrace it

i'm excited for what that path holds in store for her my heart tells me this spiritual undertaking is just a prelude to an unimaginably amazing journey i'm geeked to see what time reveals it's been one of my truest pleasures and deepest privileges to be fortunate enough to witness her make her way towards her calling and step into her truth and stand in her power my whole soul smiles at the beauty of witnessing its awakening transformation (after all, we are spiritual beings having human experiences not the other way around right)

she's a woman. anonymous. picking her way through. doing what she's designed to do as a woman. synonymous. with creating a better world for herself and others ...she's a spiritual lighthouse destined to bridge the darkness and bring peace and psychic healing and health to the souls of others

so pump-up the volume all ye ears that are listening and hearts that hear. as we turn the page. and dip into the storybook sense of awe and wonder. as astounding as any fantasy. too unreal to be real. but in reality. it really happened... and follow along as she shares the story of her strange and inexplicable encounter with noatok (and the invisible thread in the tapestry of their history) ...the trials and tribulations of her divine liberation ...and the testament and tenacity of her soul-spirit as told in her own words

pssst ...it's kinda scary to break from 'the sheep-formation of simon says' and follow the beat of your own drum i'm so very proud of you for being attentive to your 'higher-self' and endeavoring to embrace the challenge to step out of the box and live your authentic 'self'

our power of self comes from what we feel is true. our 'beliefs' create our awareness. but our vision has been wallpapered-over with spoon-fed fairytales; created and controlled via religion. culture. And societal traditions and taboos ...your gift is just a tool in your hands. and like any tool, for it to be effective. you have to use it. unrestricted by outside chatter

the best is yet to come ...i'm glad you found your door

The Sacred Messenger

—Diana Wimbish
(my mommy)

Aliya Griffin

Prologue

I've been a published urban fantasy, sci-fi romance and paranormal romance author since 2012 and as a fiction writer, I'm used to letting my imagination run wild with tales of distant planets and alien races, stories of love and romance and of triumphs and perseverance. My passion for spinning tales was born in me as a little girl and nurtured by a supportive mother who encouraged me to not limit myself or my ideas. For an impoverished, African American girl, writing had been a way to escape the existence that I thought was laid out for me. I'd often dreamt of a different life, but at that time, different felt out of reach and unobtainable with my dreams often feeling too big for this mundane and average world.

Through writing, I was able to create the worlds that interested me. I created a world where aliens invaded Earth and scattered humans across the galaxy. A world where a Black girl from Detroit was a demigoddess and Zeus's granddaughter. A world where wolf shifters and vampires co-existed. A world where aliens hunted humans for sport. Although I love the sci-fi and paranormal aspects of writing, for me, it's important to create worlds where women are able to find their voices and rise above their circumstances. In my worlds, women find their true power buried deep within themselves and the men who love them are their protectors and soulmates. In my creations, I control everything from the color of the sky, the name of the planets, the motivations of the characters, their words, actions...everything. I control every aspect of the story, from the beginning to the end. I am the Master Creator.

This book is quite different.

This book is based on real life events. Nothing within these pages have been changed or altered in any way. The events laid out on the following pages are true and happened exactly as told. As you read, it may seem that I've used my imagination to add flair or pizzaz to the story, I haven't. And trust me, this story doesn't need anything extra to make it pop. It already has Noatok, and it doesn't need anything else.

All of the recordings (except for the intuitive psychic reading session) are available on my YouTube channel (@thespiritualgirlie). The recordings aren't provided as a way to "prove" anything. They are available because I want to open the eyes of the reader/listener to the possibility of the unknown, and if listening to them helps to shed light or provide a spark of awareness in the human consciousness, I will have fulfilled the purpose of sharing my story.

But before Noatok is introduced, let me tell you briefly how I arrived to where I am today. While my journey of self-discovery has been years in the making, we'll begin this story in early 2021.

I'd just left a twenty-year marriage and moved from Michigan to Philadelphia to start my life over. My three children were all grown at this point; my oldest had a wife and son of his own and my middle son and daughter were both in college. I was unsure and afraid of what the future held for me, but I was determined to push forward and figure it out because – what else could I do, right?

After years and years of marriage and raising children, suddenly, I had all this delicious 'new-found' freedom to pursue any interest, dreams, flings, or other things I felt inclined to engage in. Problem was. I didn't know myself. I'd been busy following the bouncing ball for so long, I totally lost track of my essential identity and what drove me beyond my self-constructed role as 'wife and mother'. Somewhere between the intersection of all the heartfelt simple acts of love and joy and making others happy, I rendered myself invisible, the 'me' in 'I' simply ceased to exist. I'd left myself unattended for so long, I didn't know what to do going forward because 'I' didn't know 'me'.

It was only then that I realized how little about myself that I'd actually taken the time to know and how much of myself I'd denied self-access to but freely shared with others. That realization was one of the most terrifying feelings I'd ever experienced. A piece was missing in the puzzle that was my life, and it was me and it prompted me to take an in-depth analysis of 'self' and 'self-meaning.' Who was I ...uninterrupted? What was I? What was my origin? My reason for 'being'? My connection to the universe? What was getting in the way of what I was living for? What drives me? What are my guilty pleasures?

Most people don't know themselves and I was no exception. Getting to know myself was a seemingly simple concept but the truth was actually a whole lot more complex. In order to get with myself, to stand by myself, to stretch ahead of myself, to learn myself, to lean into myself, to be myself, I had to first find myself. And I had to travel deep in the core of 'self'—even the parts that I tried to keep a lid on and take a good *look*, straight-up, no chaser. But in order to accomplish this, I had to filter through the constant interplay of cookie-cutter chatter, aka, 'The Stepford inertia' (family, religion, society, environment, media, etc.) that was continuously being bombarded into my subconscious—sublimely programing/controlling my thought process—subtracting the authentic 'me'. Chiseling away at all those pebbles to get to the boulder of 'me' was more than just a notion but I value this me and I was determined to put in the work.

I did a lot of shadow work crawling towards that goal. For starters, I worked to heal the part of me that mourned the passing of my marriage and old family life. I worked with a therapist, I journaled, and I learned how to meditate and spend space and time in quiet contemplation with myself. I kept my self-discovery nonstructured and at a minimum. I did what felt right to do at the time I was doing it. I struck-up a friendship with myself and gave myself permission to explore life, feelings, situations and people. I tried not to take myself too seriously while at the same time, giving my innate need to know 'self' and 'self-intention' my whole-hearted devotion.

At times, it was something akin to an emotionally-delicate high-wire act and I froze, mis-stepped, lost my footing and had to go back and retrace my steps plenty of times along the way, but like the little engine that could, I took it in stride, and kept my eyes on the prize, giving myself grace through it all.

Eventually and without prompting, this path of self-discovery transitioned into a spiritual one. I'm still not sure exactly *when* it became spiritual, *just that it did*. I know *when* I noticed the path becoming spiritual, just not *when it 'actually happened'*. The first thing I noticed, was that the vibe changed from, "fun and games" to, "whoa…, who the heck am I really?" That was sometime in 2023 and by the beginning of 2024, I was in a full-blown spiritual crisis.

I've always known I was intuitive, a bit psychic, a medium (before my awakening, I'd only thought I could talk to the dead "sometimes") and was just really empathic towards people and animals. Basically, I had yet to fully tap into the magnitude of my spiritual gifts and I was blatantly unaware of the extradentary psychic energy bubbling beneath the surface of all that outside chatter.

The turning point came when I saw a past life regressionist and connected to my Higher Self for the first time. That was a goosebump moment! It was literally the first time in my life that I actually felt connected and grounded to the true essence of who I really am—and not the 'limited edition' of the 'me' encased in the human conditioning and experience of my physical avatar. When my Higher Self came forward, the strength behind its presence permeated every cell of my body, validating my alignment with myself and enabling me to finally feel the power that was 'me'. It was a profound revelation—and suddenly I knew—beyond a shadow of doubt that I was so much more than I ever believed that my soul had so much more power than this earthly plane could ever conceive.

I was so excited; I told everyone who would listen about that life-changing experience. Then, I had another session. This time, the regressionist took me to the Akashic Records and that changed everything. At the Akashic Records I was *finally home*.

The Sacred Messenger

I was welcomed there by The Keeper and gifted 'a judas-window peep' through portals and gateways to other spiritual realms and dimensions. That session unlocked something in me that turned all my psychic awareness from abstract to concrete.

Now that the gloves were off, and the veil had been lifted.

That initial introduction to the Akashic Records started to grind my gears and I found a way to return on my own accord. Blithely unaware that I was opening spiritually energetic doors that couldn't be closed, I would put myself into a meditative trance and go to the Akashic Records and hold counsel with The Keeper, lingering there, listening to the music in the silence of a magic chant meant to break a spell as he explained how time and manifestation worked and the importance of spiritual concepts.

A part of me always knew that what I was experiencing was real, while another part, the very human part, dominated by the school of familiarity and repulsed by things not understood and afraid of anything that threatened that way of thinking—was still cautiously optimistic of 'my mystic energy' and tried to chalk it up as 'over-imagination'.

Initially, I thought it was all fun and games, I felt like a child let loose in a candystore, excitedly running about, one minute in the present, next in the spiritual realm without thought nor care, rummaging through different lifetimes and other centuries, thrilling at the adventure of finding and gathering easter-egg nuggets of 'insight and knowledge' about my forever-self —until the synapsis in my brain began to become frazzled and frayed, struggling to get a sense of the world-tilting gravity of it all and the ever-growing divergence between opening up seismic rifts and trying to contain the onslaught of all its new-found elastic concepts and information, alien to my human self in this 3D world.

My mind was on fire! It felt like it was being crimped and crossed, and pushed and pulled, and snatched-back and stretched out of whack—I was afraid that it would snap. At times, I honestly worried that I was certifiably bananas. I found myself standing at the crossroads of an emotionally delicate make-or-break-issue. Something had to give. I had to make a decision.

I could stop and go back to burying my head in the sand and ignoring everything that made me, me. I knew that all I had to do was make an appointment with my doctor and afterward, I would have a prescription in hand for depression/anxiety medication and all the magical places I'd gone and the entities I'd met would be erased from my brain and I could go back to sleep and forget about my divineness.

I didn't. I chose instead to seek professional spiritual help and guidance. This was such a pivotal point in my life. Everyone who's ever achieved a measure of success in whatever endeavor they chose or that chose them, had a profound calling to stay the course, even if it cost them great discomfort or even physical pain. I was possessed with that profound calling and an unerring sense of direction. I'm so grateful to myself for being able to push past the depression and anxiety and the fear of the unknown and embrace the gifts alienated between too many ifs and make that plunge, taking small steps and giant leaps into faith. Faith, that I was finally on my true path and following my calling.

Through divine timing (tarot card readers foretold this meeting a few years before this event), I came across a video from a psychic based in South Africa, Nathaniel, from the KayNa Spirit Centre. A few months later I was enrolled in his *Psychic Development Program*. I spent six intensive weeks with him, learning to detach and look within myself which helped me learn what was me, and what wasn't. For an empath, this practice was a life-changing event.

The journey I'm on is an exhilarating start of a brand new and magical world balanced between new and old beginnings.

This path has been lonely, scary, confusing, hard, magical, wonderous, happy and fun. Sometimes I feel God shining love and light down on me, and other times I still feel as though I'm one breath away from losing touch with reality and having a full-on mental breakdown.

If this past year was any indication of things to come, my spiritual journey is by far, a long way from being over. This is just the beginning, and if this is the magic I get to experience while dipping a toe in the world of spirituality, I can't wait to see what else is in store for me!

So far, I've met a Dragon (Creator God) and my soul baby. I consider one of The Akashic Records Library Keepers a friend, whom I hold counsel with often. My faith in myself has blossomed and grown within me and the love for myself and my 'am'ness continues to expand as my place in the world is being revealed to me.

I'm not meant to be hidden. I'm to shine my light as bright as I can and wake people up. My light is in telling people my story.

Here is one of those stories.

This is the story of how my soul baby heard my cry for spiritual help and came to help me. This is a story of how I became aware of Noatok.

This book is the first of a planned spirituality collection. I hope you enjoy it and the others to come.

Aliya Griffin

Chapter One

Before getting into the thick of things, it's important to make note of how this book is written. This book is a firsthand account of an intuitive psychic empath reading, three client past life regression sessions and two of my personal past life regression sessions. The recordings from the past life regression sessions can be found on my YouTube channel (@thespiritualgirlie) for your listening pleasure. My goal in including the transcripts was so this book and the information provided, could be as authentic as possible. Client names, personal information or private information have been removed to protect client privacy.

As of right now, the intuitive psychic empath reading is not posted for public use, however, I hope this will change in the future once the client provides permission. For reason noted in Client A's section, I cannot reach out to her first (I have to obey the rules set forth by her guides) to ask permission.

The transcripts of the sessions were minimally changed to make the information easier to read. Because most of what is transcribed is exactly as stated, the sentence structure may be off. Where needed, I've updated the sentence structure, not the content, to make it more palpable to the eyes and brain while reading, but again, most of it remains original. <inaudible> is noted where, due to the client's accent and microphone, I cannot discern what was said. I've also removed most instances of redundancy in speech that we may not be fully aware of while speaking but is irritating to read in text. The most removed words are, "okay", "so", and "like".

For my intuitive psychic readings, I usually request clients to send me two pictures of themselves beforehand. One from four to five years ago and a more recent picture for the other. The pictures are valuable to me because it helps me to connect with their energy before our session. Previously, I would use the pictures to connect to the client the night before, but now, I wait until just before the start of a session to connect.

I can't explain at all how I connect, but the closest I can figure is that quantum entanglement is involved. It's a very interesting concept and while I did research (books, videos, articles, etc.) regarding this phenomenon to gain more understanding about my abilities and how they're possible, I am not a scientist and would do the concept a disservice if I tried to explain it here, so I'll leave the science of quantum physics for the professionals.

Before initially connecting with a client via a picture, I make sure to ground and relax myself by getting in a comfortable and quiet space and practicing deep breathing exercises and meditation. I then ask for mine and the client's spirit team to help assist in the connection and reveal what needs to be seen that will help the client continue on their human experience journey. I also ask to be shown what their soul's purpose and path are. Then I close my eyes and connect to the client.

I can only describe this as me mentally going through what seems like a vast darkness searching for the client. This process can take a few seconds to a few minutes. It's rather quick. So quick in fact, that if it takes more than a few minutes, I experience a small amount of panic because I can't find them. The worry is often unwarranted as I always find them, aside from a few instances. If I can't connect with a client, I've since learned not to panic because either something will happen that will prevent us meeting during our scheduled appointment time or the client's spirit team wants me to connect with them blindly.

But if all is well, I can connect easily to the client via their picture. From the client's pictures, I'm able to "read" where they were energetically in the past and how that shaped them today. I can actually do readings on clients by using their pictures alone (without an initial meeting), that's how much information I can glean from them.

From the pictures, I gain an understanding of who the client is energetically, what they've gone through, and how they're settling into the transition from the past and where they are now in their life. The information comes to me in rapid fire as words, phrases and/or random sentences. I jot it all down or speak it without trying to figure anything out or over analyzing. I take the information as it's given, relying on the client to provide context.

Example. "Sadness in the womb. Loss. Pain. Stomach pain. You felt very alone. You cried a lot. But I'm hearing you persevered." The client then relays that they had a painful miscarriage.

Usually, this process takes about twenty minutes where the client and I are discussing the roadblocks they've faced and overcame in the past and how their life is now, as they've progressed along their path. We discuss the changes they've been through and areas that still need adjusting or issues that need to be resolved in order to move forward.

Once I get the information needed from the pictures, I then ask for the client's and my spirit guides to let me see what the client needs to see. This presents as a vision of some sort. When I say "vision", I mean a true psychic vision. My eyes can be open or closed, it doesn't matter, because the vision is in my mind. I'm usually given a vision that cannot be taken literally and needs to be unpacked. I might see the client in a whirlwind, fighting the wind while being tossed and tumbled about like a rag doll. I might see different color strings tangling around their stomach, arms and legs. The client might be standing on a hilltop, the weather gray and dreary, or the client may be in a field of beautiful flowers on a bright and sunny day.

Whatever is presented to me, I take it all in, reflecting what I see, noting every detail, down to the color of their clothes, the emotion that's triggering me or the smell of the air. It's important to look at the entire scene, down to the miscellaneously placed objects (a flower, pendant, etc.), sounds, colors, feelings or taste, because it all symbolizes *something,* and I want to make sure the client has everything they need to understand what their guides are telling them.

So, as you can see from the above passage, connecting to the client a day before our scheduled session can leave me tired and energetically drained. Hence, why I now connect a few minutes before sessions.

From the beginning of my intuitive psychic reading session with Client A, I knew this wasn't going to be a run of the mill intuitive psychic reading. All sessions are conducted over the internet, using a meeting app. I prefer that the client as well as myself, turn the cameras off. I'm reading their energy, not their body language for these sessions. When the sessions are complete, I provide a recording to the client (barring any technical mishaps that may have occurred).

After the introductions and pleasantries, I began by explaining my spiritual gifts; that I'm a psychic, medium/channel and empath, and I informed the client what she could expect during the session. I find that explaining my spiritual gifts helps the client to understand any of the "weirdness" coming from me that they may witness. By the time I get through explaining this (within the first five or so minutes, after the pleasantries of greeting each other), I'm probably already displaying some of the "weirdness" that I've told the client about.

For me, it's important to explain the communication issues that I might experience throughout the session only because I'm self-conscious when my speech becomes altered. Some of the communication issues I experience are disorientation, slow speech, voice dropping an octave, trouble finding my words, trailing sentences or sometimes I'll abruptly stop talking for a few minutes. So, you can see why it's important to explain these issues to the client, otherwise, I appear to be going through a serious medical event, and I don't want the client to be concerned about any of this during the session.

Once I addressed the communication and speech issues, I then informed the client of what they can expect from me as a psychic, medium/channel and empath. For my psychic abilities, I explained that I can "see" the past, present, future, as well as past lives (if there are lessons that need to be learned in this life from a past life). Sometimes, my visions can be taken literally, "I see you celebrating a new job" or the visions cannot be taken literally, "You're in a vast ocean, drowning and land isn't in sight", and we have to unpack it to find the message. Since clients are seeking me out for an intuitive psychic reading, they're pretty onboard and expect this aspect of my gift and because of this, this explanation goes rather smoothly.

As a medium/channel, I receive information from whoever's on the other side of the veil who'd decided to step forward. But oftentimes, I don't know who from their spirit team I'm channeling. The "who" actually doesn't matter, we're all energetically connected. If a particular spirit wants to be known, they'll present themselves accordingly. I've learned to just go with the flow and expect the unexpected. Well, I've learned this with every aspect of my gifts. But oddly enough, having spirits, entities, guides, etc. pop up in my psychic readings isn't disruptive. I'll be chatting along, in the zone, then out of the blue, I'm asking the client about the random man in a suit that's showing up to our session.

I explain my empathic abilities last because there are certain instructions for my clients that they need to be vigilant about during these sessions, and since I want them to remember them as we move through the session, I don't want the instructions to be lost.

When I connect with a client, I'm connecting with them in all ways. Most people know empaths experience what other people feel but don't understand that this means *all feeling*, not just surface level (sad, happy, scared, angry, etc.) human emotions. If the client is happy, I'm happy. If the client is nervous or anxious, suddenly so am I, but what most people don't understand about empaths is if the client has so much as a slight headache or something as obscure as right knee pain, that's what I'll experience while connected, as well.

While not in sessions, if I experience random feelings or pains, I'm able to discern what is me and what is not. The random knee pain? Yeah, I'll try to own it as mine for a few minutes, but I've learned a trick on how to know what's me and what isn't. If there's no context for the feeling or sensation, it's not mine and I let it go, which effectively releases me from the abnormality. But while connected to clients during a session, I can't always easily figure these things out.

The only reason I can think of for this (not being able to easily figure out what is my mine or someone else's), is that when I have one foot in the 3D world and the other in the spiritual realm, I'm not totally connected to my body. I can feel and experience what's happening within my body, but I'm not *totally* connected to it. Because I'm here, but not really *here*, it takes me longer to figure out what's me and what isn't.

This is where I enlist my client's help. I'll ask the client to take note if I begin rambling about random ailments which often sound like, "My right knee is hurting. I don't know why my right knee is suddenly throbbing. Why is my knee hurting? It's quite achy." To me, I sound like a little old lady interjecting my random complaints throughout the session. If the client notices this behavior coming from me, I've instructed them to stop and figure out what's going on within their own body and if what I'm experiencing is theirs and not mine, to let me know. Once they let me know, I'm then able to easily disconnect from those feelings and let the feelings and/or sensations go and move on. Otherwise, the client will have her recording peppered with my random complaints.

Whew! That's a lot of explaining to unpack, but luckily, this usually only takes about seven minutes to get through. Afterward, we're ready to move into setting our intention for the session, then move right into the reading.

Now, let's get started. Check your blind spots and buckle-up.

Chapter Two
CLIENT A
Intuitive Psychic Reading: 23-JUL-2024

The entity who entered my life revealed a few names to me; Noatok, Noa and Acturu. For this book, I'll refer to him as Noatok as that's the name that resonates when thinking about him.

The first time Noatok revealed himself to me was during a very interesting intuitive psychic reading. This was my first encounter with this particular client who I'd virtually met through a past life regressionist group that I was a member of. I'd put a call out to the other group members, asking for volunteers who wanted a *free* intuitive psychic reading (At that time, I was learning how to interpret my visions and wanted more practice reading people and trusting myself). While we were figuring out our schedules, I learned that the client had received previous guidance from another psychic who'd told her that she was on an epic adventure complete with a talking mouse.

For those of you who don't have experience in dealing with the spiritual realm, hearing about talking mice may be something that would throw you for a loop. Me? I was excited to learn about her adventure because as a psychic and medium/channel, this wasn't the weirdest thing that I'd heard that month, let alone that week.

Aliya: Now, just, like, all of a sudden... I'm gonna hit mute for a second, just so I can figure out my throat. (a few minutes later...) Okay, I'm so sorry. I just had to clear my throat all of a sudden. Really urgently.

I rambled for a few minutes about my throat, which I don't add here. I do put the client on hold as I clear my throat so I can move on with the session without being uncomfortable.

Usually, at the start of each psychic reading session, I experience some type of throat issue which normally presents as me needing to clear it. I'm used to this, and I've figured it's my guides clearing my throat chakra to start the session. If the throat issues progress or present as something other than mild irritation, I know intuitively that the client is having some type of issue with how they communicate. Here, I don't have enough information to go on at the first instance of throat problems, so, I have to wait to receive more information from our spirit team.

Client A: You are just fine.

Aliya: We're going to speak into our water, and you'll repeat after me.

We both spoke the intention directly over a glass of water.

The Intention for my Intuitive Psychic Readings is:

Source Divine, please bless this connection. Please allow us to see what needs to be seen and know what needs to be known, as we continue on this human experience journey. Please welcome any guides, ancestors, and spirits who are present to help us. Please block and protect us from those with any ill intent or plans to do us harm. Most importantly, when our session is complete, please allow us to fully disconnect from one another and leave this connection lighter, brighter, and happier than we were when we first began.

Aliya: One other thing that I did forget to tell you is I'm still learning what works for me. (In all of my previous sessions) I connected (to the client's energy) the night before and ask their guides to send me any kind of advice, wisdom, or what have you.

Then I would ask for a vision. This was all (done) the night before. Then I'd (have to) carry their energy with me to the next day. And so, I'm trying to play with that a little bit more.

I didn't connect with you yesterday. I didn't connect with you at all until we first got on the phone. That's probably why it was so intense for me a little bit there. I've been creeping, creeping, and creeping closer to the session to (energetically) connect. This is my first time connecting with a *BAM*.

I rambled some about my initial feelings and pulled up her pictures so I could read her energy.

If you could just let me know why you decided to come today? Like, what piqued your interest and if you've seen psychics before? And anything like that.

Client A: No, I haven't. I did have a spiritual activation reading not too long ago and also, I thought that was very interesting. Also, I would like to know my Spirit Guides. I haven't... I don't feel that I'm connected with them. I know they're there, but if that's supposed to be... Also, in that reading that I got, there was a map given to me in the ethers, and I don't know what that's about, and I don't know if that's something that you would be able to give information on. It might be hidden at this time. And—

Sometimes, while the client is talking, I receive visions and downloads, and other times I'm able to fully listen to their reasons. While it may seem rude to stop the client while they're explaining why they've contacted me, I've already received everything that the client's soul and/or guides want me to address with the client and I want to get into it because we are bound by time (the psychic sessions only last one hour).

A spiritual download is a sudden, intuitive influx of divine wisdom, insight, or knowledge that comes directly from Source (Source/Divine/God), higher consciousness, or one's higher self. It often feels like receiving a message, vision, or deep understanding all at once, without needing to analyze or logically process the information. These downloads can come in many forms—I experience them as a flood of thoughts, a strong inner knowing, and sometimes through dreams, symbols, or even physical sensations. Downloads often arrive unexpectedly during meditation, moments of stillness, or even during everyday activities when my mind is relaxed and open.

Unlike traditional learning, which happens through study and experience, a spiritual download bypasses those steps and delivers a profound truth instantly. It's as if my consciousness tunes into a higher frequency, allowing me to access wisdom beyond my current awareness. These insights may relate to personal growth, universal truths, past or future events, or even creative inspiration. The key to working with spiritual downloads is trust. Since they often arrive without immediate context, it's important to write them down, reflect on them, and allow their meaning to unfold over time.

Aliya: You can stop there. And we'll just get on with it. So, I had a lot of visions while you were talking. I'm sorry…

I often have this obsessive need to apologize for the impaired speech, although I've already given the client all the information needed to understand what's happening with my speech and why.

So, my feet are very hot. My feet are hot. They're to the coals… Like…my big toes. I just wanna jump. I just… I'm having a hard time not jumping. My big toes are just wigging out here. And…and you're leaving. You're gonna…there's something about you leaving. And I apologize because it's (the information) just coming.

And so, for my visions. I'm all over the place today. So, maybe I should not be waiting to like, the moment of, to connect <laughter>. So, there's a lot going on right now, and I did forget to mention that with my visions, some can be taken literally, but we'll get the idea of that and some things.

I suddenly went right into a vision. My eyes were open, but I no longer "saw" the human 3D world, I was in the spiritual realm.

There's a fire. A fire to the right of me, like…like, a blinding light to the right of me.

What I need to work on is giving up control. Our spirit team had given me a vision, a strong one at that, and instead of going with the flow, I'd stopped the vision in order to provide an explanation of how the visions come for me.

I'm trying to hurry up this part (of explaining my visions and how I see things). So, they (the visions) can't… They shouldn't all be taken literally. If I say, you know, I see you in a dark cave. It doesn't mean that you are going to be in a dark cave anytime soon. Yeah, it just means a dark place. Okay? So, as I'm firing out these, I just want you to…

Client A: I can handle it.

Aliya: Okay. But oh, maybe… The… okay, maybe that's the sun. I'm sorry. I started with a couple of visions here. My stomach is…very… I don't… I don't know why. I'm a little nauseous there. I'm trying to focus on one thing at a time. So…your chakras are being aligned. Are you doing grounding?

The vision left when I pulled away, then I became hyper-focused on the new sensations coursing through my body.

31

Client A: Yes, I'm barefoot a lot outside.

Aliya: Oh! That's why all the feet sensations. Why were they hot? Oh! They were hot because of the grounding. Yeah, it's working! Like, when you're out there, do you feel, like, the sensation, like, I feel the sensation of it's so much, like, my feet are twitching. It's so much, do you feel like that when you're out there?

Client A: Yes, I feel energy in my body very well.

Aliya: Oh! Oh! That's the mark!

Client A: I have, like, energy charge in my body very well. Does that make sense?

Aliya: Yeah, because I feel it now. And since I'm not... I don't do that, so as you remember, I said, I'm an empath. So, everything that you're feeling, I'm feeling. I just... I didn't know how to explain it. Just all these sensations. But I'm like, pressing my... I have a grounding mat that I put my feet on just to make sure that I'm grounded during these (sessions), and like, the sensation is... Normally, I don't feel anything (while grounding on the mat), but I feel the vibrations from this mat. But my whole... My feet are activated, and then I feel that when you do that, you align your chakras. That is your source of power.

Client A: I feel this energy in my body, and I felt like I use it on my partner. He knows, he knows about it. It's like, a healing, or it's something...

I had a vision of her holding her hands out and energy zaps leaving her fingertips. As I was seeing her hands in my mind, I held up my own and studied them, feeling and seeing the energy in her fingers coursing through mine, needing to get out.

Aliya: In your fingers. That's where it's (the energy) leaving. It's leaving through your fingers. It's (the energy is coming in) through your feet and the source leaves through your fingers. Okay, okay, that was a lot. That was a lot.

Okay, I'm trying... I just... So, when I do it the day before (connecting with the client's energy) I can write all of it down. But now that I'm getting it (in real time), I have a pen in my hand

I'm in the 3D and *in the spiritual realm, and myself here is confused and trying to figure out what to do with this pen in my hand.*

I don't know why I didn't think that I was... Just that energy charge, that must feel wonderful all the time. I would do it all the time. There was - such a rush.

Client A: Yes.

Aliya: Now that I've come down from it, it kind of leaves me, like...maybe not a headache. I wouldn't say a headache. Like a current zaps through you and now you don't have that, you know what I mean? Now it feels like you dropped, but you didn't really. That's what it's feeling like. A little bit like an adrenalin rush. And then the threat (rush) is over, and now you're back to regular. That kind of energy.

Since Client A identified the sensation, I felt as hers and not mine, I was then able to pull out of it. Pulling away from the sensation allowed me to return back to the vision I had for her.

Okay. What was I saying? To the right of me. It was red first. It was bright red. I'm trying to see if I can pull that (vision) back and see if there was anything there that you needed to know. So, it was bright red, and I thought it was a fire. I didn't know there was a fire to the right of me. But then, as I turned my head to see what I was looking at, it became like an orange-ish color, or just yellowish like. (a question I was asking myself) Did I recognize that as a sun? And then I kept going. Then it was a bright white light. I'm just trying to figure out if that means something.

Let me see, let me think about it for a second.

I read the energy from the vision and tried to figure things out.

Is there bad news? You thought it was bad news? But you're slowly thinking now that maybe it's not so bad? I don't think you're at the part where you know it's better (yet).

This was a vague question for the client, but I'm also just talking through my vision, trying to figure it out.

Client A: Maybe so.

Aliya: Is that, is this resonating?

Client A: Yeah, kind of.

Aliya: Okay, you can let me know what that is.

Client A: My daughter told me that was pregnant a few days ago. That's only really.

Aliya: I don't know if that's it. Because I'm not really picking up on that. Usually, when you're talking, I'll hear things that need to be said about the topic. I don't really think that's it because I was listening, and I was hearing things, but not really around that topic. It was kind of like a yay or nay, it was... It wasn't really here or there.

I experience certain sensations that help me to understand which direction the conversation should flow. If the vision had something to do with her daughter being pregnant, I would have gotten a tingling sensation either in my feet or abdomen (which I call, "hits"). But as she was telling me about her daughter's pregnancy, nothing happened.

Client A: Does it have to do with anything about my boyfriend's back?

Aliya: *Hmm...* I'm getting the feeling it's not something small. Again, if it doesn't resonate, if it's not right, then, you don't have to... We're not trying to make anything fit. But it just seems like, first I was...

So, I'm gonna repeat it. Just in case you have to listen to the tape, you know, next month, or a year, you can close the loop on this.

It's very hot, like I can feel the heat. And because of that, I said, it's a fire. Now, I'm getting the word "childhood".

But anyway. As I turned, I saw that it wasn't such a bad thing, that blinding red light was actually like, the sun's rays. Like, it's going to be okay. But it's slow... It's not a fast turn. It's like I'm slowly turning my head. So, that means the time between these (the different points of light that I saw) are going to be slow. But then, as I get past the sun's rays, which are good, and I feel good about... I looked over, and there was just blinding, shiny, bright light, and I just knew it was even better than I thought it could be.

That's really all I'm getting from this. I think because I had that energy surge, and I was onto something else. I'm just trying to recall.

I'm thinking it was something that maybe happened a while ago that you're slowly (coming to realize). So, this is just (something) for you to think about later. That you're slowly coming to know. It took me a while to get there. But coming next, is for you to realize this is the best.

I don't know what "that" is. But I'm now hearing, "Spans a lifespan." So, yeah, I'm thinking something is already in motion. That light at the end was so beautiful. When you think about it later and you remember, then I just want you to know, the outcome is so much better.

Client A: Very good.

Aliya: Usually, I start with the pictures. Before my intuitive psychic readings.

Although I've learned to expect the unexpected when dealing with spirits, I still have a duty to the client to not let the session go totally off the rails. I pivoted to reading the energies from the pictures she'd emailed me to get the session back on track.

But again, I'm just all over the place (with this reading). Now, I'm going to your pictures. You in 2020... Wow, such a drastic change! Well, I wouldn't say a drastic change. You were...I want to say, never shy, but I, as I say that, I think sometimes (you were shy). But in 2020... Let me see if I can focus on that. You were confident. (You're) Still (confident), but now your confidence is on one hundred.

There was a few minutes pause as I tried to figure out the energy between the two pictures.

All I'm getting is that something happened between these two (pictures). I'm just trying to figure out... I mean, because of course something happened (between 2020 and 2024). Did you have a baby? Just that my womb is very activated right now. Does that resonate at all?

Client A: My daughter had a baby a year ago.

Aliya: I'm a little confused.

Not by what she said about her daughter or boyfriend, but by the two conflicting energies from her pictures.

Because it's... You're so... Well, the best way to explain this, is that these energies don't match. I mean, they're both beautiful energies, but... So, whatever event it is, it's making my womb activated. It feels like, now something has clicked into place. So, you're saying nothing went on with you in-between here (2020 to 2024)?

Client A: No.

Aliya: *Hmm…* Usually, I will look at the first picture, then write down what I see. Then, I'll look at the second picture, and write down what I see, and then you know, your Guides fill in the blanks of like, those middle years.

But with you, what I'm having trouble with… I can look at the first picture, see a person. Then look at the second picture, and they (the person in the picture) look kind of alike, but then energetically, they don't look alike. It's freaky, how different that these two energies do not match. And then, I'm just getting pulled to the middle.

I was transfixed with staring at the email and the blank space between the two pictures in it. In the email, the pictures were organized one on top of the other. And no matter how hard I tried, I couldn't "unsee" the space between the pictures. There was nothing significant about the pictures or the space between them, but her guides wouldn't let me let it go.

So, something happened in the middle (years) that caused this. Huh! I don't know. I'm sorry. I don't know how to explain that. But I'm fixated on it. Usually, I can move on if something doesn't resonate. But I'm fixated on something (the space between the middle of the pictures) because your guides won't let me *not* be fixated on it. I don't know why I'm also getting (hearing), "misaligned". Just misaligned over and over again. Which is also confusing. Because you, when I first channeled you, I felt you aligned.

So, I'm just trying to. Oh, so I'm just now getting… I'm getting with you…

I received a download from her guides that I'm trying to understand.

I'm still here, I'm sorry… Are you spiritually attacked?

Chapter Three

Client A: No. I don't think so.

Aliya: Has anyone ever told you that?

Client A: No.

Aliya: I'm so sorry. But this is very odd. It's like I'm trying to pin a thought down. I don't like telling people that they aren't supposed to know something or like, if there's a blockage there. Because then I don't know if it's because I can't see it, and you know, you're not supposed to know, or if it's truly that you're not supposed to know.

Client A: Yeah.

Aliya: So, I mean you're there, like you're there. But there's a trickster there, too.

In my mind's eye, I saw clearly a little dark-haired boy who had the appearance of some type of Native American decent. He was between four to six years old, and he was looking at me with a mischievous gleam in his eyes and had a hand covering his mouth. He was snickering and had a really cute, playful energy about him.

The feeling I got was an overwhelming sense of playfulness, but also a trickster energy. Not trickster in a way that made me mistrust or be wary about him, but an energy of fun. My first thought at seeing him was, "He's here to help." And I'd erroneously assumed he was here to help Client A through whatever the vision was signifying for her. A happy and playful energy began to course through me as I'd connected with him (At the time, I didn't know that I was connecting with him) which would noticeably last for a few days after this session.

39

Client A: Oh, yeah?

Aliya: Yeah. I can't pin it. I can't pin you down. This isn't like, definitely not like harmful or negative, nothing like that. I don't want you to think or walk away from this, thinking that.

The energy began to turn very mischievous. The trickster was letting me know that I wouldn't get the information I sought or that something was being hidden from me.

Client A: I don't feel negative.

Aliya: Yeah, nothing negative. It's nothing like that. I just feel (and see his energy) like a little kid holding his hands in front of his face and giggling, like a little sprite. I don't know folklore like that. I don't know (what) a sprite (is). That's (the term that just) came up.

Client A: I think I know what a sprite is.

Aliya: Okay, I don't know if it's, like, maybe Irish. I don't know, but a little sprite came into mind.

A sprite is a mythical or supernatural entity often associated with folklore and mythology. The term generally refers to a small, ethereal being or spirit, similar to fairies, elves, or other magical creatures. Sprites are often depicted as light, airy, and mischievous beings that inhabit natural settings such as forests, meadows, or streams. The word "sprite" comes from the Middle English term sprit or sprit(e), derived from the Old French spirit (meaning "spirit") and ultimately from the Latin word spiritus, meaning "spirit" or "breath." Over time, the term came to refer specifically to magical or otherworldly beings in European folklore. In literature and art, sprites are often portrayed as guardians of nature or playful tricksters, sometimes helpful to humans and sometimes causing minor mischief. Sprites continue to be a part of modern fantasy and popular culture, often representing the magical and whimsical aspects of nature.

Aliya: Let's go a different route. I'm sorry. Let's go a different route. I'm gonna try something else. I just find it interesting…

At this point, I was confused by the energy of the little boy and although I wasn't trying to get around him, I knew that I couldn't. I felt that the little boy wasn't going to give me the information that I was looking for. I wasn't angry with him. It didn't feel like I could ever get angry with him. It just felt like…this was game. All a game. And he was happy that I had joined. I felt that he was an assigned helper, helping her along her journey. He was here to make sure everything was running smoothly and staying in line. But he would definitely make sure to have his fun along the way.

Okay, so this is very, very good. I'm sorry for you, because usually they're (the spirits/entities/guides that come through) like, very good and I'm telling people what their soul needs to hear, but this is very different for me, because I am new (at doing personalized intuitive psychic readings for clients).

I'm psychic and have known I was since I was a young girl. Up until the beginning of 2024, I'd only read family and friends for fun. But at this point, I'd been reading professionally for four months.

I don't know what's what, and I'm picking up on different energies here.

Although, I was able to see the little boy, I wasn't aware that he was "real" and not just part of a vision.

Last week, I talked to a dragon *(YouTube: @TheSpiritualGirlie, Past Life Regression 12-SEP-2024)*. So yeah, I mean… It's very good (that we're experiencing a "sprite" during this session). You're strong. The connection was like, BOOM. Then, I felt the energy pulsating around you. That came up very, very strong. But then, even the first vision, it was kind of iffy. I saw it clearly, but I was having a hard time figuring out what it actually meant.

So, we had to step through that and then, now your faces (from the two pictures) don't match energetically, and I can't focus on anything else. That is also… Well, what the heck is going on? That hasn't happened (to me before) and then me seeing a little kid laughing and then just the words, "a sprite"? So, with all that, you said that you had… Did you tell me that you had something spiritual happen to you? Like a spiritual awakening?

Client A: No, I had a spirit activation session.

Aliya: Okay.

Client A: She entered into my energetic field and spoke to my Higher Self and found out some… I was… I am a creator of rock people, like golems.

A golem is a creature from Jewish folklore, traditionally described as an animated being crafted from inanimate matter, such as clay or mud, and brought to life through mystical or divine means. The concept of the golem originates from Jewish mysticism and is most closely associated with Kabbalistic traditions. A golem is typically created by a learned rabbi or mystic who uses sacred texts and rituals to animate it. Golems are usually created to serve and protect the Jewish community, often in times of peril. They can perform physical tasks, defend against enemies, or carry out their creator's commands.

Unlike human beings, golems lack free will, emotions, or independent thought. They act solely on their creator's instructions, often to the letter, which can sometimes lead to unintended consequences. In modern culture, the golem frequently appears in literature, art, and film as a figure representing creation, power, and unintended consequences.

Aliya: Okay.

Client A: One of my other incarnations was named, Kara. She was proficient in making golems. They're usually made with clay, but my Higher Self specifically said for me, I would use rocks, and I could use them in the ether. There was also a mouse that she spoke to, and he laid out a map on the table and said it was for me, and it wasn't for him to explain it or...

Aliya: <laughter> Oh, okay.

Client A: Or for Sage to explain it to me. And it's a journey. He said, I'm gonna have to have a steadfast heart and something else. I can't... It's not coming to my head right now.

Aliya: Oh, okay. Okay, so it made me feel good to hear that, like, physically, I felt really good. It felt magical. So, a couple of things. When I asked you... What did I ask you? If someone was attacking you or put a spell on you? It was... I'm sorry. I'm holding this pen here, and I haven't written anything down but "misaligned". So, obviously this (me taking notes during the session instead of before it) doesn't work.

I just remember asking you that because I felt like there were spells around you, and not so good spells. But when you're saying that you're making the golems... I meant that... I don't know about the golem, but that's what you were told. But that's what you did with your hands. You made spells and not so good spells, and by that, I mean they (the spells) hurt people.

Client A: Oh!

Aliya: And so, I just thought that (the negative spiritual energy) was you, because it was *in* you. So, I just misinterpreted that, because I did see that in you.

Client A: Yeah, I've never done that in this lifetime.

Aliya: Yeah, yeah, yeah. It's quite okay. I don't want to lose this thought… I don't want to lose either thought. So, remind me to go back to the mouse. You're gonna have to remind me.

Client A: Okay.

Aliya: Okay, because I can't hold onto both thoughts. But with this past life, and maybe that's what we were supposed to be talking about, and sometimes it takes me forever just to go around (visions) and if they show(ed) me the easier route, it would be so much better.

As mentioned in the explanation of my spiritual gifts, I can pick up on energies from the client's past lives. Sometimes, it takes the client's help and a lot of mental gymnastics on my part in order to sift through the energies I'm experiencing while connecting to the client.

But, with our past lives, we bring them with us, what's needed, to this life. I have a lot of past lives that I've brought here with me and that's because I needed them in this life. And it's like we're activating right now because my feet are doing that same thing over again (vibrating with energy).

I was actively receiving "hits", meaning, this is the right topic that we're meant to discuss, per Client A's spirit team. This is where her spirit team stepped up, giving me downloads as messages to give to her.

A spiritual download is a sudden burst of information or insight from a higher source—like my Higher Self, Spirit Guides, or Source. It's not something I have to figure out; it's more like the knowledge is dropped into my awareness all at once. It can come through as words, images, emotions, or just a deep sense of knowing. Sometimes it feels like remembering something I've always known, while other times it's a light bulb moment where everything suddenly makes sense.

So, that's one life or two lives that you brought here for a reason. Apparently to do this ultimate quest that actually is not even spanning this lifetime, it's spanning over *lifetimes*, is what I'm being told.

Hmm! I see (a vision) the mouse with the map. You *are* on a magical journey. I love these.

I absolutely get a kick out of psychic sessions that take an unexpected turn.

You have a lot you're doubting, though and that's normal. I'm not gonna be able to convince you of this, but the words you still need to hear. But you are...you're on this journey. It's a journey that you chose. It's (the Guides) saying, *"Not many people choose this route."* You did, though.

So, when I was telling you about my vision of the fire, it (the initial journey) did start off hard. But you're at the midpoint now, this (current) life is at the midpoint right now. You still have many lives to finish it (the journey). But the reward is what you signed up for.

There's no cheating involved. Help is along the way. But then also, you don't need the help, but help is along the way. I think that's it, something else might come (later). Were you told anything like that?

Client A: No.

Aliya: Okay.

Client A: That's good. I was told that I was a timeline reader.

Aliya: Oh, yes. This is part of the game that you've chosen. The first thing that came to mind is...what is that movie? It's like a really old sci-fi movie and they're like, *The Hitchhikers of the Universe.* That one.

Client A: Okay.

Aliya: Have you ever seen it?

Client A: I'll have to go back and watch it again.

Aliya: Yeah, yeah, it's like, I think it's *Hitchhikers of the Universe*.

What I was thinking of was The Hitchhikers Guide to the Galaxy.

...or something like that. It's a very campy, sci-fi movie. But in it, they're hopping, they're hitchhiking across the universe. And so, they're picking up things along the way. This is kind of how this game operates. So, I would see you... Yes, you would have to be able to read a timeline, because... Oh! Maybe that's...

I was saying that it takes a long time for me to turn and see it (the vision). That's the journey, but it's also a timeline and you have to be able to read that and suss out. But the lives before (at the start of the vision where I described the fire) weren't so good. And you are very cynical that you've carried from past lives.

Client A: What does that mean? Cynical?

Aliya: Just like, "This stupid game. This...*ugh*." It's wearing on you. Like, you don't know if this is going to pan out, so you're trying to be optimistic, but it's kind of like *ugh*. So, but...

When I'm connected to a client, I'm opening myself up to receive any information that their spirit team present to me. Although, they can sometimes derail a reading, I just go with it because there's information the spirit team thinks the client needs to hear at that specific time.

I just remembered something, going back to when you asked were your Guides present? I'm so sorry, I lost it that quick. It was a yes, but it was something else attached to it. Because then I started thinking about the mouse with the map, because when you said that, I clearly saw the mouse, and I saw the map.

The Sacred Messenger

Client A: Heart is what I said, steadfast heart, and something else.

Aliya: It wasn't that. I am so... Oh, my God.

I'm frustrated at not being able to untangle what was being presented to me.

What's coming is, just adventure. I've already told you that this is an adventure, like a quest. *Hmm!* I like this for you. So, going back to your pictures, because now I see. Without looking at your pictures, I see them in my head, and I see what they're doing. I do understand now. They aren't representing this life. These are two separate lives or... Oh, okay... I'm so sorry, I keep.... I know I keep apologizing. I'm apologizing. I should have been...

Client A: It's fine.

Aliya: I should have been writing this down yesterday, and now it's coming, and it's okay. So, bear with me now. We had to go through all of that for you to understand this, is what I'm being told.

That top picture, the one from 2020, that was a different half of a life, or lives. The bottom picture is this current one (life) and going forward. I hate to say it like that, because time isn't linear at all. So, when I say going forward, that just means the next life. Not like going forward in time, but just the next life, which could be in the past. That's why I couldn't make my mind see the same person, because they were two completely different people.

When most people think of "past lives", they think of a life they've lived in "the past" from the current linear timeline. But from a higher-dimensional perspective, all time exists simultaneously and from that perspective, a past life can take place in the future with the understanding that our souls are not

47

bound by a linear timeline. Our souls exist beyond the constraints of physical time and can incarnate in what humans perceive as the past, present or future. Although the future past life hasn't happened yet in the human linear understanding, it still exists from the soul's multidimensional view. (If you're interested in this concept, feel free to listen to the following past life regression sessions where the client experiences a past life set in the future (YouTube: @TheSpiritualGirlie, Past Life Regression 25-AUG-2024).

Again, what I'm being told that means, is that you're halfway through the game, and that's why I kept staring at the halfway mark (the space between the two pictures). And I was telling you that there was a top picture and there was a bottom, and I'm staring at that middle point. And I could not get un-fixated from that middle point, because something happened (during that time) and it kinda clicked to align. And '*misaligned*' was the only word that I wrote down.

Oh, my God! This took a strange turn, didn't it?

Client A: Yes.

At this point, everything that I'd seen and heard clicked into place. Once everything clicked into place, I got a really warm and good feeling throughout my body, and my thoughts became clearer. My communication issues usually subside at this point, as well.

Aliya: That's why we met, which is funny, I think this is hilarious, but that's why we met.

Source had previously explained to me that I'm a lighthouse and spiritual bridge. During this particular period in my life, I'm an energetic bridge between the 3D world and spiritual realm and the people who find me (by following my light) will be at the precipice of a spiritual transformation, in the midst of one or freshly out of one. Of course, this will not be the case for everyone who books a session with me, but when I encounter one of the souls I'm destined to help, it makes me beyond excited. It honestly feels as though an energetic ding rings and the feeling is electric.

So, you're at that halfway point. The game gets better from here. You've done the hard part. It gets better from here. You're activating, and you do need to (activate with) the Earth. With the red clay, is what I'm hearing, and that's probably why.

Now, going back to point one, which we started like forty minutes ago, when my feet were going crazy touching the earth (the grounding mat). You said the golem was made from clay. That's why they told me to talk about the lives. So that's why you brought that life here with you. You needed to activate with the Earth's clay and that's how you do that in this life. You are one powerful being. You need to be outside activating feet on the ground. That's the skill you pick up from this life to move forward.

Client A: Nice.

Aliya: Okay. That took a strange turn, and I was all over the place. It all, just kind of circled back around in a strange and weird way, but it was just, whew!

Any questions? And it's okay. I'm being told, because you're still like, you're not there. And I told you before, I may not convince you of this now.

While I could feel the client being onboard with I was telling her, there was still lingering doubt. I'd wanted to stay on the topic and go over it again with her, but her Guides were telling me that it was okay, and she would get it later.

So, you do need to keep this recording because you are gonna start to get it. Things will come and they will reaffirm

49

what you're doing. But for this lifetime, it isn't gonna make or break if you believe this or not. Even if you decide and you're like, you know what? That was crazy. I'm gonna not believe that and I'm just a regular person. That is okay.

Client A: Oh, I'm not regular. I can promise you that.

Aliya: I'm just saying, like, we talk ourselves out of stuff. That is okay. But what you are (meant) to do in this life, and why you brought that past life with you, and there's many more, but you'll learn those as you go along, as you pick up more skills. But right now, you are activating your soul. You're using the Earth's crust. So that is the skill that you are picking up (in this life).

Client A: What am I supposed to do with that? I'm like, kind of at a crossroad right now, not crossroad, but I am retiring. I've been a hairstylist for thirty years now and I'm partially retired, and I'm kind of, you know, into all this woo-woo esoteric stuff. I love it.

Aliya: Yeah, yeah.

Client A: I think it's great like, I wanna help people, like, with their inner child and stuff like that.

Aliya: You can do anything with that (the energy she grounds from Earth that courses through her body and releases through her fingertips). You are picking up a very powerful skill that you need to, that you are—

Client A: What is the skill?

Aliya: The skill is that you are… You do magic with your hands and the reason that you can do magic, and I'm like looking at my fingertips (while I speak), the reason that you can do magic here is because you are picking up all that energy from the Earth's crust.

Client A: Yeah.

Aliya: So, that's why you need to be out there grounding. You're storing up all that energy, and you are doing magic with your hands. This is a skill that you're learning here (in this life). It's a skill that's gonna continue to grow as you pick up more, not just through this lifetime, but other ones too. So, you are not at a crossroads, but you are at that middle point here. But I understand why you would feel that way because I was very fixated on the middle (part).

Client A: I'm not sure what to do with what I feel inside of me. That electricity you felt. I feel that and I can activate it and sometimes... I've given people hugs and just like, *hmm*, like push that love through them, and they absolutely know or like, are in shock and I'm just smiling <laughing>, yeah.

Aliya: You're doing what you're supposed to do. And I understand what the question is. So, what you're supposed to be doing, is practicing harnessing that energy. You can't keep it (in your body). You need to release it, is what I'm being told. So, make sure that you are releasing it, and it sounds like that's what you're doing. But I know what the question is. The question is, "What do I do with it in this life?" I'm not getting any answers about what to do with it in this life, because I'm looking at the game.

Client A: Right.

Aliya: So, that's... I see this huge picture of like, just a plethora (of information) and I'm having a hard time scaling it (down). I know what you want to know. Like, "What do I do?"

Client A: Well, maybe it's not for me to know right now, and just keep...

Aliya: Or just, you can do so many things. Maybe what you do with it in this lifetime really doesn't matter, but you learning it. If you wanna be a healer, if you wanna do this, if you wanna like, be a, you know... I don't know why I'm getting this vision of a televangelist like, shocking people and healing them, like, whatever. It's up to you. I'm seeing the bigger picture and it's you acquiring skills.

Client A: Right. Okay.

Aliya: And this is the skill here. You do have to practice, and they want you to practice. The door is wide open. I don't honestly see (anything else). And that's rare for me to say that. It's rare for me to say, that, "The door is wide open." Because when I see something, it is what it is.

Client A: Right.

Aliya: And there's no deviation. But with you, I just said, *"The door is wide open"*, because you're not a normal player of this (game of life). You're a different player.

Client A: What kind of player is she? <laughter>

Aliya: Right. So, you're a different player. And so, my vision is kind of distorted. I'm just, like... I'm getting, *"Seer through veils."* Have you started seeing things yet?

Client A: No.

Aliya: Okay, that's gonna come. You're gonna start hearing things, too. Now, this is in this lifetime I'm talking about. You're gonna progress quickly, I'm hearing. But it's okay, because you are a tough cookie. I think that's... No cheating. But I cause I... I was...gonna... Oh! I'm having a hard time even thinking of what I wanted to tell you, because I'm... I'm... There's no cheating at all, is what they're telling me.

I was still receiving downloads (medium/channeling) about what's going on with her but now experiencing difficulty in speaking the words to tell her. Being connected to the spiritual realm oftentimes can be draining, depending on who I'm in connection with and for how long. Here, I've been connected to that little boy (sprite) energy for an hour which is why I was tired energetically and was having trouble maintaining the connection.

Client A: What does that mean, no cheating? I don't... I'm not a cheater.

Aliya: I wanted to give you more information, like (tell you) who was giving me the information. And I'm having a hard time articulating that, and all I hear is, *"No cheating."* I think I can remember this when we disconnect. So, I'll email it to you.

Spoiler alert: I did not remember the download.

Okay. It's very… This is… This is the strangest thing.

Before disconnecting and going our separate ways, we had a brief personal conversation about her journey and her path moving forward. The little boy gave us instructions that I relayed to her.

1. I am able to help her but have to follow the game rules without cheating.
2. Client A is able to reach out to me for help, but I'm not able to reach out to her.

The Guide said that there will be times when she believes she's in an epic game and the other times she will not. If I were to reach out to her, that would not only remind her that she's in the game, but also provide her with confirmation. But if she reached out to me first, then she is fully aware of who and what she is (an epic gamer) and as long as she remembers herself (without my prompting), she can receive my help.

3. Also, I cannot charge for my services.

At first, her Guide said that she could come to me once, but then he said my help was an open invitation. We did laugh about this because in order to receive my help, I'm unable to charge her. Charging her would be considered cheating because she would be paying me to help her.

Our session ended with me excited for the journey she's on and wishing her luck. I am very curious as to when I'll hear from Client A again and what would prompt her to contact me for help.

This was the first time I saw Noatok (the little boy who'd I'd mistaken as her Guide and Sprite).

Aliya Griffin

Chapter Four
CLIENT B
Past Life Regression: 22-AUG-2024

I met Client B, a young woman possibly in her mid to late twenties and of Hispanic descent, in a spirituality group that I'm a part of (this group is run by my spiritual mentor and the person who helped guide me through tapping into my psychic abilities). I'd recently completed a ten-week Past Life Regression certification class and needed volunteers for practice.

After our pleasantries, I'd asked her what I'd begun to ask everyone, "What made you decide to have a past life regression?" Her reply was that she wanted to learn about herself in *this* life. Apparently, she'd recently discovered that when she was about five years old, her had taken her to a shaman to have her spiritual gifts removed. When she'd finally asked her father about it, he'd confessed that at the time, he'd felt her gifts were too powerful for her and needed to be removed for her own safety.

Client B expressed that she didn't have a recollection of ever having any kind of spiritual gifts or even what those gifts might have been, but she'd wanted to visit Source or her Higher Self to see if her gifts could be re-activated, if possible. This was right up my alley. If I could help her to understand herself, her spiritual gifts and possibly help her on the journey to re-claiming them, I wanted to.

At the start of the past life regression, it's important to spend at least thirty or so minutes getting to know my client and understanding their motives and expectations for the session. Although, after our talk, I instruct them to release all expectations, I find it necessary to know them just the same. My reason being, once we're in the past life or lives or if we're visiting the spirit realm, I want to stay true to what's important to the client. And although I have a list of their questions intended for Source or their Higher Self, I want to be able to ask any follow-up questions that I think may be relevant and important to the client.

After reviewing her questions and expectations, I determined the best course of action. For this session, the client and I had decided that we would (in this particular order) visit a past life that most connects to the client's current life, review that life with her Council of Elders, seek advice and have her questions answered by Source then visit the Akashic Records Library. While this is how we hope to progress during our time together, I remind the client that anything can happen once we enter the spirit realm.

During this time, I also make sure they understand the difference between hypnosis vs. trance. Though the two share similarities, the difference between hypnosis and a trance-like state lies in the level of structure and intent behind each experience.

A trance-like state is a natural and often spontaneous mental state. Through imagery and relaxation, I help the client shift their focus inward, helping them disconnect from external distractions. Trances can occur without formal guidance and are often associated with activities like meditation, daydreaming, or creative flow. In a trance-like state, the client is in a state of altered consciousness, but it's typically less structured. The client usually feels detached from time and space or deeply immersed in their inner experience.

At the time of the publication of this book, I'm not trained in hypnosis, which is a guided process led by a trained practitioner (or self-guided in some cases) to access a deeply relaxed and focused state of mind. It is a structured practice designed to bypass the conscious mind and connect with the subconscious.

While hypnosis is often used as a tool for transformation, healing, or insight, a trance-like state is more free-form and can occur during many activities. Both are valuable states of consciousness that help access deeper layers of the mind, but hypnosis is intentional, whereas a trance may simply be an organic moment of presence and connection.

The script I use to talk clients into a trance is pretty long and takes about thirty minutes to get through. Because of that, I'm not adding it to this book. The script is a combination of scripts provided from my past life regressionist course, and bits of pieces of lines from guided meditations that I listened to online that resonated with me. The script focuses on relaxation, calmness, silencing the mind and ego and guiding the client's consciousness through the veil of the 3D world and into the spiritual realm. The transcript for all of the past life regressions going forward uses that same script and the transcription picks up at the end of it.

For additional context, the past life regression sessions are three hours long. Roughly thirty minutes are spent discussing expectations and the plan for the session with the client, then another thirty minutes to talk them down into a deep trance-like state with the actual regression lasting about an hour and forty-five minutes. The last few minutes are reserved to bring the client out of the trance, then I spend the remaining time grounding the client back to the 3D world by briefly reviewing what we experienced.

The grounding is important because the client usually wakes up from the session somewhat confused at being returned back to their life on Earth. Also, the reason that we don't spend longer than two hours in the spiritual realm is because while the client is resting comfortably during the session, their spirit is working very hard to energetically travel and visit the places that we explore. This is very tiring to the soul and mind. All clients (including myself) experience this tiredness.

Reader take note: Since you're reading the transcripts of the past life regression recordings, it may seem like the conversation is flowing at a regular talking pace. This is not the case. The clients have long pauses between words and sentences and even a minute or two pause before the clients answers my questions. Their speech is slowed as well.

Aliya: You're now standing at the brink of the portal. So welcoming. The air within is shimmering and beckoning. Your soul is smiling with knowing and familiarity. So familiar. So peaceful. Take a deep breath. Leave your human form behind, let your soul rise and step through. Through this portal of light are all the stars and all the worlds and all the lives you have ever lived. And all the lives you are yet to live. All the loves you have known and are yet to know. All your family, here and now and then and when. And all and everything you have ever known as any being and any non-being.

And so, you float into the light, and find yourself in a space so vast, with colors so clear and beautiful and unique that they are yours, and yours alone. And as you float, you feel so safe, so warm and so very comfortable. You are traveling to the most relevant time. You are traveling to the most necessary place. Moving through barriers of where you thought you could go no further. You move through barriers of where you have never been before. And never before imagined, you could go.

And you do, because you can. And you are the very essence, of this movement and light. You are finally arriving, here and now, to the most relevant time. Arriving here and now, to the most necessary place. And as the movement slows, you begin to gather your bearings. And as the movement stops, you begin to feel your point of view. I want you to tell me, the very first things that you see or, the very first impressions that you have as you begin to understand, where you are, and what is happening around you. Tell me, what do you see in this new space?

Client B: Right now. I'm just standing in a field.

While viewing a past life, the client will describe the experience in first person. Their consciousness immediately recognizes them, as them—a piece of their collective soul.

There's usually initial moments of confusion because suddenly, the client went from being "them" to now being "them" in a different time and place, which, as you can imagine, is very disorienting to their human brain.

Aliya: Okay. What is the weather like?

I prefer to ask them about the weather if they're outdoors because I find that it "grounds" them to the scene.

Client B: Clear, sunny.

Aliya: Is there anyone there with you?

Client B: Not that I can see. But I feel like someone's looking at me. I don't see anyone.

The fact that she couldn't see anyone but could "feel" being watched intrigued me, but I would come back to that later. First, I wanted to see if she was human or something else.

Aliya: Okay. Look down at your hands and tell me what they look like.

Client B: Can't really see them.

Aliya: Why can't you see them?

Client B: I feel like I'm in the field, *and* I'm like in space.

Aliya: It feels like you're in the field, or that you're in space?

Client B: And that I'm floating in space.

Aliya: Where did the field go?

Client B: Okay, I'm there again.

Aliya: We're going to stay in the field. Look at your hands and tell me what they look like.

Client B: They look like my hands.
Aliya: So, female?
Client B: Yes.
Aliya: Can you look down and see your feet?
Client B: *Mm hm.*
Aliya: What do they look like?
Client B: Barefoot.

After establishing that she might be human, it was time to move on to establishing a time period.

Aliya: What kind of clothes are you wearing?
Client B: I'm wearing a type of, like, a cloth dress.

Now, it was time to re-visit the lurker.

Aliya: Can you look around and see if you can locate who is watching you?
Client B: A child.
Aliya: Okay. And whose child is that?

Since we hadn't yet established an age for her, I didn't want to assume who the child might be to her. But I find when I ask about family, the client instinctively know who the people around them might be, especially if there is a deep emotional connection them.

Client B: I don't know, but he doesn't… It's like, I think it's a boy. He doesn't seem scary. He seems friendly.
Aliya: He seems friendly? Okay.

This was the first indication that the child might not be a mere "child". Most of us wouldn't look at an unknown child and the first thought we had about them was associated with fear. I was wondering why she would think a child was scary. But since we hadn't yet established an age for her, she herself could have also been a child looking at another child. And as a child herself, she might have the mindset to determine if they were scary or not.

Aliya: Can you go over to the child?

Client B: Okay.

Aliya: Let me know what happens when you approach the child.

Client B: (The child is) Like, hiding behind some tall grass.

Aliya: Is he hiding from you or playing with you?

Client B: Playing.

Aliya: Okay. Do you know this child's name?

Client B: No.

Aliya: On the count of three, you will know this child's name and who he is to you. One. Two. Three. Who is this child?

Memories of the past are housed in the recesses of the brain. By prompting the client, I'm helping them to unlock the memories of their past lives. Usually, this works about 80% of the time and the client is able to easily recognize (read and know) different languages as well as their past life name, age, family and year.

Client B: I'm not sure.

Aliya: Is there anyone else around you?

Client B: No.

Aliya: Where are you?

Client B: I'm not sure, it doesn't seem familiar.

Aliya: We are going to now move to an important day of this life. An important day that you need to see in this life. On the count of three, you will be there. One. Two. Three. Tell me what you see.

Client B: It's like I'm in a square, like a town square and there's people working. Feels like I'm in like, the olden days.

Aliya: What do the houses look like?

Client B: Stone. Stone buildings.

Aliya: Where are you located?

Client B: At first, I felt like I was somewhere abroad. But now it feels like, I'm like, here in the States.

Aliya: And what year is it?

Client B: I wanna say, like, the late...the eighteen hundreds.

Aliya: Can you look down at your hands again and tell me what you see?

Client B: They're like, White female hands. I'm wearing like, a long skirt and my boots.

As mentioned above, Client B is Hispanic. The hands she described now were not the same as she described before. When we moved to an important day, we should've stayed in the same life. While it's "supposed" to work that way, I've learned that anything dealing with the spiritual realm doesn't always work how we humans think it should, and the client can, in fact, jump lives without me prompting. So, while this wasn't what I'd expected, her jumping to another life wasn't unexpected.

Aliya: How old are you?

Client B: I want to say late twenties.

Aliya: And how do you feel right now?

Client B: Confused.

Aliya: Do you know why you're in the town square?

Client B: Well, when I first came in, I felt like...people were running and rushing. But now that I'm here, it feels calm.

Aliya: Look around and see if there... If you have a feeling that you should be somewhere or go someplace.

Client B: I see the child again.

Curiouser and curiouser. In no way, do I make the connection of who this child might be. Remember, at this point, I'm not aware that the "sprite" I'd seen months prior was connected to my soul and not to Client A's epic game. I'm only curious here because it was obvious to me that we had jumped lives and in doing so, we should've left the little boy in the previous life, not taken him with us to the new life she's viewing.

Aliya: The child is there again?

Client B: He's peeking from behind the wall.

Aliya: Does he look the same as he did before, or different now?

Client B: I don't remember what he looked like, but he feels familiar.

Aliya: Can you go to him?

Client B: Okay.

Aliya: What is he doing now?

Client B: He's looking up at me and I'm looking down at him. I'm not sure if he... I feel like he wants me to follow him. But then we're just standing there.

While it's not necessary for a past life regressionist to have any spiritual gifts, I find that since I do, I'm able to intuitively guide the client through their lives and help them to uncover trauma that needs releasing. I'm also able to astral project during these sessions and sometimes I'm right along with them as they're experiencing this journey.

Through my connection, I saw a little tan boy with big eyes and a bright smile holding his hand up to me (as the client). My body felt calm and pleasant being near him and I knew that I would be safe. In my chest, I felt like following him was not only the right thing to do, but something that I needed to do.

Aliya: Let him know that you will follow him. But as you follow him, narrate what you see and what is happening.

Many clients don't remember parts or most of the past life regression and since I don't know which information will be retained, I try my best to have the client vocalize what they're seeing so they'll have the information for later (provided via a recording).

Client B: I keep getting visions that I'm following him, but then, that we're also standing in the same place.

Aliya: I'm giving you Source healing now. So, you can do what needs to be done. To see what needs to be seen during this vision. We're activating this Source healing so you can do what needs to be done and see what needs to be seen. What is happening now?

Client B: I'm following him.

Aliya: Okay.

Client B: I'm walking down the street. There's a wall to the left, a stone wall. And to the right, there are houses. It's early evening. I can hear my boots on the stone ground.

Aliya: What is his name?

Client B: So, in the other one. The first time I saw him, for some reason, I got the name Noatok. And now here, I got the name John, and then, Noah.

Chapter Five

Aliya: Is he talking to you?

Client B: No, he's just walking.

Aliya: Can you ask him where he's taking you?

Client B: Yes. He doesn't say. He just wants me to follow him.

Aliya: Okay. What is your name?

Client B: < *Client's name in her current life* >. It feels like I'm coming back.

I hadn't taken much notice that she'd answered her own name since she had a common name and one that would've been appropriate for that time period.

Aliya: You're coming back. Where?

Client B: To Earth.

I believe that by answering her own name, Client B began losing her spiritual connection.

Aliya: I want you to stay where you are and go back. Go back. We're going to put you back into the into the town square. Maybe you are not meant to follow him right now. Are you back in the town square?

Client B: Yes

Aliya: Let us fast forward or go to a day that most connects that life, to this life. On the count of three, you will be at a scene that connects that life to this life. One. Two. Three. What do you see?

Client B: Feels like I'm floating in space. *Concentrate.* I see the field again.

Aliya: Okay, good. We are going to move you to the scene that most connects that life to this life. On the count of three, you will be there. One. Two. Three. What do you see?

Client B: Field. And it feels like, like a Native American tribe.

Aliya: Okay.

Client B: I see like, huts. It's a village. A community. I see the little boy again. He's in one of the huts peeking out. I'm going to him. He's smiling.

Although we'd obviously jumped back to the first life, I wasn't certain if this was still the first life or now a third life. But I was very curious about the presence of this little boy who'd jumped multiple lives with her.

Aliya: Let him know that you can't hold this space. He will need to tell you what you need to see.

Client B: He took my hand and I'm following him.

Aliya: Okay, tell him, thank you.

Client B: Thank you.

Aliya: Ask him what he is to you.

Client B: He's smiling at me, but he doesn't say.

Aliya: Okay.

Client B: But he feels like we're related.

Aliya: Where is he taking you?

Client B: To the middle of the...middle of the campsite, and there's a fire...a campfire. A big campfire.

Aliya: What do your hands look like here?

Client B: I'm the same age as the other girl, but they're more tan or brown.

Aliya: Like, you're a member of the tribe?

Client B: *Mm hm.*

Aliya: Where has he led you? What do you see?

Client B: I see the campfire, but it's big, but I don't feel the heat. I just see it. It's larger than me and there's the other inhabitants, and they're just going about their day. Some of them are noticing us.

Aliya: What do you need to do in this space?

Client B: I don't know. I feel confused but safe.

Aliya: We need to know what he is trying to show you or tell you.

Client B: There's a man looking at me. I think he's a Chief leader.

Aliya: Okay.

Client B: I'm not sure if I should approach him, but he's staring at me.

Aliya: Can you ask him why the little boy has brought you here?

Client B: I'm going to go up to him. He wants to talk to me.

Aliya: The Chief?

Client B: Yeah.

Aliya: Okay. You can talk to him.

Client B: I'm going inside of his hut. I'm not sure what it's called.

Aliya: Narrate the conversation so that you can remember it when you wake up.

All of the past life regressions are recorded and a copy is provided to the client. The information the client is receiving is often overwhelming and downloading into the client's brain fast and furious. There is no way for the client to remember everything and it's important for the client to be able to review the recording for insightful and invaluable spiritual information they may need later.

Client B: They're like… It's like, he's not talking English.

Aliya: What we're going to do, is I'm going to send you Source healing. Send you Source healing in your mind to unlock the language that you already know how to speak fluently. On the count of three, you will be able to understand him. One. Two. Three. What is he saying to you?

Client B: *Hello, <Client's name in her current life>! Welcome. It is nice to see you here.* Thank you. Why am I here? What does this mean?

While communicating with the Chief, Client B oftentimes asked her question in her own voice and her answers were directly channeled responses.

Aliya: Speak up just a little, please.

Client B: Why am I here? What does this mean? He's just staring at me.

Aliya: Okay.

Client B: *You do not need to be afraid. You are safe here.*

Aliya: Can you ask him where *here* is?

Client B: *Here is a community. I'm not where you're from. We are in another planet.*

Aliya: Okay.

Client B: *There is peace here. Calm. Unity.* The boy is next to me again.

Aliya: Can you ask him what planet this is, and why you were brought there?

Client B: What is the name of this planet? And why am I here? *The name is Unknown. You are here to say, Hello.*

Aliya: We're here to do what?

Client B: *Just say, hello.*

Aliya: Oh, that's nice! Who are these people to you?

Client B: The boy feels like he's my son and the Chief feels familiar, like an old friend.

Aliya: Is this where you come from?

Client B: Is this where I come from? They're both smiling at me. *Perhaps.*

Aliya: What are...

Client B: *It is one of many.*

Aliya: What is the name of these people?

Client B: What is the name? What is the name of these people? *Iowate (I-O-wat-ay).*

Aliya: And the little boy, will he be your child in your current life?

Client B: They're both smiling at me again. They're not saying anything, but I'm feeling like yes.

Aliya: Is this a spirit world or is it a real place?

Client B: It feels like a real place even though I can't see everything clearly.

Aliya: Ask him if he knows why your (spiritual) gifts were blocked.

Client B: Do you know why my gifts are blocked?

Client B: *You were not ready for them. It was too much for your young brain.*

Aliya: Can you ask him, if they were too much, why did you have them?

Client B: *It was a gift of your family, from your father's side.*

Aliya: Can you ask him, what needs to be done in order for you to be ready to have them unblocked?

Client B: …block my gifts… *Be patient and focus. Learn to go within yourself more. Be sure of who you are and why you are, and it will be revealed.*

Aliya: Okay.

Client B: The little boy is holding my hand and smiling.

Aliya: You can…if you feel that you can, and you want to, you are able to give your future son love and acknowledgement and let him know that you will see him soon. He seems very excited to see you in this space. It's okay to be emotional. It's a very emotional time. Ask the Chief if you are able to visit again to receive learning and knowledge?

Client B: He says, yes, this is my home.

Aliya: That's your home? Okay. How do you connect with your home?

Client B: How can I come back here? *Do the same practice through meditation. The more you do it, the stronger you'll be, and the easier the path will be. We are here.*

Aliya: Is that your tribe?

Client B: I think so. Yeah. Yes, I would like to say, yes.

Aliya: Ask the Chief, is there anything else we're supposed to be doing in this session, right now?

Client B: He says, he's happy I'm able to gain access here. There is much more for me to see. *In due time.*

Aliya: Okay, good, very good. They hijacked your past life to tell you this. So very good.

Client B: What does that mean?

I didn't answer that question here, as I didn't hear it, but she asked the same question during our debriefing. I told her that hijacked meant that the little boy kept taking her from the life we'd thought she needed to see and had taken her to her spirit family instead.

Aliya: Ask him, we were going to go to... let's see... We were going to ask Source questions and go to the Akashic Records. Ask him if that is okay for you to do now?

Client B: <inaudible> *Yes, you may.*

Aliya: Is there anything else that you want to do here, while we're here or any questions you want to ask him?

Client B: Well, I wanted to look around, but when he told me that, he stepped to the side, and I saw like, a portal open up behind him and he's guiding me towards there.

Aliya: Can you ask him where the portal leads? Tell him that you trust him. <laughter> The practitioner just has to know where you're being led to.

While this session had taken an unexpected turn and I was confident that we're protected spiritually and neither the Chief nor the little boy had plans on doing us any harm, I felt it was necessary to protect the client during her journey into the unknown.

Client B: Where does this go? *Your other lives.*

Aliya: Tell him, thank you. Which life do you want to see now?

Client B: Whichever is ready to reveal itself to me.

Aliya: Okay, very good. Now step through the portal and you will be there. What do you see now?

Client B: I'm still floating in space.

Aliya: Okay, at the count of three, we will be at a life that's ready to reveal itself to you, that you need to see today. One. Two. Three. What do you see?

Client B: A jungle.

Aliya: What is around you?

Client B: I don't know if this is like, one of my Spirit Guides that's affecting this.

Aliya: Why do you say that?

Client B: Because this is where he's from.

Aliya: Who?

Client B: One of my Spirit Guides.

Aliya: And why do you say that?

Client B: Because I've never jumped to the jungle like this, and I don't know. It feels familiar, and I feel like this is where he's from.

Aliya: And when you say "he" who is "he"?

Client B: My Spirit Guide. One of my Spirit Guides.

Aliya: Where exactly are you?

Client B: A tropical jungle.

Aliya: Look down at your hands and tell me what you see.

Client B: I see the hands of a woman. Dark skin.

Aliya: Okay.

Client B: I'm barefoot again.

Aliya: Is anybody else with you in the jungle?

Client B: My Spirit Guide.

Aliya: What is your Spirit Guide's name?

Client B: I'm not sure but he's tall. He's not saying anything. He's just there.

Aliya: Can you ask him why he has brought you here?

Client B: Why am I here? He wanted to say, hello and I am welcome. He wants you to know that he is here whenever I need him.

Aliya: Thank you.

Client B: Thank you.

Aliya: Can you ask him how many lives he has been with you?

Client B: How many times have you been? It's no answer. Three.

Aliya: Three?

Client B: I don't know. That number came up. Three.

Aliya: Ask him how you can connect with him more.

Client B: Dreaming. In my dreams.

Aliya: Okay.

Client B: And just talking to him as if he was here.

Aliya: Have you ever seen him before?

Client B: I've heard of him.

Aliya: You've heard of him?

Client B: When he was revealed to me, that he was with me. They described him to me.

Aliya: Okay, tell him thank you for revealing himself to you.

Client B: Thank you.

Aliya: And ask him where you should go next.

Client B: <inaudible>

Aliya: I can't hear you anymore.

Client B: Where do I go next? Can you help me access that information? He says to just keep walking through the jungle.

Aliya: Okay. Tell him—

Client B: And a path will appear.

Aliya: Tell him, thank you.

Client B: Thank you.

Aliya: And walk through the jungle. Let me know when you see the path. You are safe. You are on an adventure.

Client B: I see a path

Aliya: Okay, follow that path.

Client B: The trees are fading away. I see a lantern. A streetlight. Street lantern.

Aliya: Okay.

Client B: I'm wearing the boots again.

Aliya: You're wearing the boots again?

Client B: *Mm hm.*

Aliya: Okay. You're back where you were before?

Client B: Yes, but it's like in that same world, but a different part of the town.

Aliya: Okay.

Client B: No. It's nighttime.

Aliya: Do you have a sense of what you need to do here?

Client B: I'm near a dock, near the water. I see boats, fishing boats. I hear the horn of the boats.

Aliya: Okay.

Client B: Looking around. Everyone's just going about their business, walking. I don't know. I don't know why I'm here.

Aliya: Let's move you forward to an event in this life that you should be aware of. You are moving forward to an event of this life that you should be aware of at the count of three, you will be there. One. Two. Three. What do you see?

Client B: Space, again.

Aliya: On the count of three, we are going to go back to the town square. One. Two. Three. Are you back into the town square?

Client B: Yes, it is evening, and I see the clock and there's bells that are tolling. The bells are tolling.

Aliya: At the count of three, you will be standing outside your place of residence. You will be standing where you live in this life. One. Two. Three. What do you see?

Client B: I see a door. There's a fountain in the middle of the square, and there's houses surrounding it. There's doors.

Aliya: Is that where you live?

Client B: I think so.

Aliya: Okay.

Client B: Let me go inside.

Aliya: Yup, go inside and tell me what you see.

Client B: The little boy again. He's on the table eating.

Aliya: It seems like he has been with you for many lives.

Reader, take note of the revelation that the little boy is her son in this life. This point will be discussed at the end of this book.

Aliya Griffin

Chapter Six

Client B: Yeah. I'm looking outside. <inaudible> It's a beautiful view.

Aliya: Is there anyone else in the house besides you and the little boy?

Client B: There's a guy in the kitchen.

Aliya: Who is he?

Client B: I think he's my husband.

Aliya: Does he feel like a soulmate or just another soul?

Client B: Just another soul.

Aliya: Okay.

Client B: He's cutting up some bread and the little boy is eating his meal.

Aliya: Okay.

Client B: Another little girl is running <inaudible> on the stairs.

Aliya: Okay.

Client B: It's his sister.

Aliya: Oh, okay. How do you feel being in this house?

Client B: Feels nice, it feels comfortable.

Aliya: What do you do for work in this life?

Client B: What do I do for work in this life? Let me see. I think I'm a housewife.

Aliya: Okay.

Client B: A writer, no trying to see…mend clothes.

Aliya: Okay.

Client B: Not sure.

Aliya: Okay.

Aliya: On the count of three, we are going to fast forward to a time where you are much older in this life. One. Two. Three. What do you see?

Client B: Little boy's a teenager now.

Aliya: Okay.

Client B: So is his sister.

Aliya: What are you guys doing?

Client B: They're just standing in the kitchen slash living room.

Aliya: Okay.

Client B: They're getting dressed, or they are dressed. He's fixing his tie or his clothes—

Aliya: Okay. Oh, go ahead!

Client B: I think we're going to a celebration.

Aliya: What are you celebrating?

Client B: I think we're just gonna go to a festival, a town party.

Aliya: Okay.

Client B: Everyone is dressed nice.

Aliya: Now, we are going to fast forward to the last moments of this life. On the count of three, you will be in the last moments of this life that we are viewing. One. Two. Three. What do you see?

Client B: I'm in a bed. My son is sitting next to me, holding my hand. He's caressing my face.

Aliya: How old are you?

Client B: I'm old. I have gray hair and… Eighty-nine.

Aliya: Is your daughter there with you?

Client B: She wasn't. But she is now.

Aliya: Okay.

Client B: She comes and goes, but she doesn't come inside. She just stands by the door. He's the one that's there the most.

Aliya: You can let him know that you know who he is to you and that you will see him again soon and that you are connected for always and you can let <the past life's name> know that you are there with her, and now, we will be present with her as she takes her last breath and releases the soul. What do you see now?

Client B: She's gone. He's crying. He's sad, but he accepts it.

Aliya: Does the soul stay for a while and linger with the body or does the soul leave?

Client B: Just leaving.

Aliya: As we leave, we are going through space. We are floating through the spirit realm, and at the count of three, you will be in front of Source. One. Two. Three. Tell me, what do you see?

Client B: I see a bright, white light.

Source will present in a way that's most comfortable for the client. Although it presents most commonly as a bright, white light, I've had sessions where Source presented to the client as a tree, the wind and even as Morgan Freeman. Yes, thee *Morgan Freeman!*

Aliya: How does it feel?

I think it's important for the client to know how Source feels so they can recognize it on their own.

Client B: Feels massive. There's like a…like a glass castle behind it.

Aliya: Oh, okay.

This piqued my interest. I'd never heard of someone describing a glass castle behind Source. And as she said it, through astral projection, I was able to see it in my mind's eye, as well. It was a big, beautiful magical place that was out of reach to us. It felt like a place we would be able to get to one day, but not right now. A place to desire to be.

Client B: Very beautiful.

Before each past life regression session, I instruct the client to come up with at least ten questions for Source (or their Higher Self, if that's who we're channeling during the session). We also spend a considerable amount of time reviewing and going over their prepared questions. I want to understand why the question is important to the client and what the client is hoping to gain from the answer and this experience. Knowing this also helps to negotiate with Source or their Higher Self if either refuses to answer a question. If that happens, I can follow up with, "<insert client's name> wanted to know because blah, blah, blah." And Source or their Higher Self can reply with their reasoning as to why they won't answer, etc. That in itself is helpful to the client as they're usually being provided with an issue that needs fixing/addressing. There will be instances of this negotiation process noted throughout this book.

While communicating with the Higher Self or in the presence of Source, the client will oftentimes ask their question in their own voice but answer as a direct channel and address themselves as a third person (she/her or use their name).

Aliya: Ask Source, what gifts were locked away?

Client B: Source, what gifts were locked away in my body, my mind and my soul? *Clairvoyance. Seeing. Seeing souls. Communication with past souls.*

Aliya: Ask Source, how many lives you have led?

Client B: How many lives have I led? At first, I heard three, and then I heard, far too many.

Aliya: Ask Source, how can you have far too many and three (lives) at the same time?

Client B: Now I see the number ten or thirteen.

Aliya: Ten and thirteen.

Client B: No. Three, so thirteen.

Aliya: Ten, thirteen, or three.

Client B: Yes.

Aliya: Are those numbers all meant to be together?

Client B: Let me see. Three, one, three.

Aliya: Three, one, three. Okay, three hundred and thirteen lives?

Client B: I think so. Yes.

Aliya: Okay.

Client B: Cool. I had to shiver.

Aliya: Ask Source, what gifts can be unlocked today?

Client B: What gifts can I unlock today? Source is asking if I am ready. If I am sure.

Aliya: That's a question for you.

Client B: Yes, I am ready. *Clairvoyance. Communication.*

Aliya: Okay.

Client B: *Knowing.*

Aliya: What was the last one?

Client B: *Knowing.*

Aliya: Okay.

Client B: And then something about seeing souls, but not yet.

Aliya: Let Source unlock those, with the understanding, giving you only as much as you can handle at this time. It can be unlocked. <a minute later> Has Source unlocked those gifts for you?

Client B: I see like a…like, you know… In the banks, when they have, like, the big silver locks? I see one of those being shattered.

Aliya: Okay.

Client B: There's light coming out of it. And it's surrounding me.

Aliya: How do you feel?

Client B: I feel good. Just it was really bright.

Aliya: I am going to ask Source if there are any gifts that I can have unlocked?

During our initial consultation, Client B was made aware that I would most likely have a few questions to ask Source while we were connected. This is a practice that I generally take with all clients. While standing in the spiritual presence of Source or another divine being, I never pass up the opportunity to open myself up to receive any divine guidance that they might have for me.

Client B: My head hurts a little bit.

Aliya: Giving you healing energy. You just received a lot of information. You have healing Source energy in your head, surrounding your brain, providing comfort and peace and safety.

You don't need all the information right now. It can come to you in waves, as needed when you can handle it. So, we're not locking it away. We're just going to turn the tap so only a little bit comes out at a time as you can handle it. Does that feel better?

Source healing, in a spiritual context, is the process of connecting with the universal, divine energy of Source itself. It involves channeling Source's pure, transformative energy to heal and rebalance the client on multiple levels: physical, emotional, mental, and spiritual.

In practice, Source healing is used to restore harmony within the body's subtle energy systems. During transformative sessions like a past life regression, where deeply buried memories and latent psychic gifts may emerge, the sudden influx of heightened energy can sometimes overwhelm the client.

For example, when Source unlocked Client B's powerful psychic abilities, the intense energetic shift manifested physically—as a headache. Source healing was called upon to gently integrate these new energies to help to relieve discomfort by reestablishing equilibrium and ensuring that the emerging gifts were balanced and supported.

Ultimately, Source healing is seen as a way to realign one's energy with the divine blueprint of the soul. By fostering a direct connection with Source, it empowers individuals to navigate their spiritual transformation with greater ease, ensuring that even challenging symptoms are met with the restorative, loving energy of the Divine.

By prompting the client, I'm able to guide the client to call on or activate this God-like healing within themselves. It's not proven by science and could very-well be a placebo-like effect, only making the client "believe" they are receiving healing from some outside force. But for me, it doesn't matter. What matters, is that it works and works immediately. The client will immediately feel better when prompted to activate it.

I cannot explain Source healing in such a small passage and any description that's not totally devoted to an entire book would be a disservice. I would encourage the reader to research Source healing and its use in spiritual healing. We all have the ability to Source heal ourselves because we are part of Source itself.

Client B: Yes.

Aliya: Okay, good. Those are your gifts. You can access them when you need them, and when you're ready, you just have to turn the tap to the right so that more comes out. Do you understand?

Client B: Yes.

Aliya: Okay. Again, I'm going to ask Source if I have any gifts that are locked, that can be unlocked today?

Client B: I just got the word, clairvoyance.

Aliya: Source, please unlock the clairvoyance for me today. I am ready. Did Source unlock that gift for me?

I understood that Source wasn't truly unlocking the gift, as Source had previously confirmed I already had this spiritual gift. But during this session, Source had decided that I could open the tap to increase the clairvoyance abilities that I already had.

Client B: Yes.

Aliya: Thank you. Can Source let us know what generational trauma needs to be addressed and released for you?

Client B: Please reveal to me what must be known. *Woman's suffering. Woman silenced. Women diminished. Accomplishment and growth.*

Aliya: Is that how you can release that generational trauma, live, accomplish, and grow?

Client B: I believe so.

Aliya: Okay, good. Thank you. What is your purpose in this life?

Client B: *To heal. To learn. To prosper. To learn to be by yourself and that's how you will find your answers.*

Aliya: How can you use your gifts to serve your purpose?

Client B: *Accessing them will help you grow and understand yourself and others.*

Aliya: What should you do to be able to learn your gifts?

Client B: *Meditate. Practice. Pray.*

Aliya: You said, pray?

Client B: Yes.

Aliya: When will she meet her mate in this current life?

Client B: Soon.

Aliya: Soon? What is his name or the name of the mate?

Client B: Some reason the name, Jonah.

Aliya: Jonah. Soon. This is a question for me. What steps do I need to take to build my spiritual practice to thrive and help everyone?

Client B: *Keep practicing. Keep growing. Keep healing. Work from the kindness of your heart and connect.*

Aliya: What does that mean, "and connect"?

Client B: *Connect with yourself and others and connect with me.*

Aliya: Can Source tell me the name of my soulmate?

Client B: The first name that came up was, Sébastian.

Sébastian would be my soulmate's soul name, not his Earthly human name.

Aliya: And when will I meet him?

Client B: *It is not known.* I see this spinning… I don't know, just spinning.

Aliya: What's spinning?

Client B: It's like spinning pictures, but I can't make out what they are. Like, I don't know, I just get the sense of spinning.

Aliya: At the count of three the pictures will stop spinning and you will see. One. Two. Three. The pictures have stopped. What do you see?

Client B: I can't see them.

Full disclosure. Although I'm psychic, most of my future is hidden from me. I've been aware of this for quite some time. Source and my Spirit Guides had previously explained that since

I'm a powerful psychic, my Higher Self had hidden certain pivotal events that would occur during my lifetime in an effort to guide me into having a more authentic human experience. However, I'm able to see snippets of my future, so not everything is blank. Source will provide me with guidance or a hint though if I have a specific question.

Aliya: Does Source have any advice for you today?

Client B: *Keep taking this journey, this path.*

Aliya: Are there any secrets that Source can tell you today?

I don't know where I picked this up, asking Source/Spirit Guides/Higher Self for a secret. But I figured, why not? Maybe we haven't asked the right question, or I've missed the point about something, but I always feel that there may be something, anything, that the spirit team wanted to secretly reveal, and all they need is a little nudge from me.

Client B: Are there any secrets that Source can tell me today? I just see the glass castle.

Aliya: You just see the glass castle?

Client B: Yeah.

Aliya: What does it look like?

Client B: It's like reflecting different colors. Many colors, graphic.

Aliya: Do you get a sense of what it is?

Client B: Feels like another world.

Chapter Seven

Aliya: Can you ask Source, if you're able to visit that world today?

Client B: He says, not today.

Aliya: And what is that world called?

Client B: Source, what is that world called? It just gave me a headache.

I've tried since to visit this glass castle but can only view it as I had during this current regression. And no matter how hard I try; I couldn't move forward energetically. This castle (which felt like another realm of existence) still eludes me and although it was a place shown to the client, I hope that one day Source will open this castle up to me.

Aliya: Just gave you a headache?

Client B: Yeah.

Aliya: We're going to give you Source healing. We're gonna heal your head. All that Source energy is healing your head. You're standing right in front of it so it's so easy for your head to feel so much better. Does it feel better?

Client B: A little bit.

Aliya: Tell Source, thank you.

Client B: Thank you, Source.

Aliya: Okay, we are going to move forward now to your Council of Elders. At the count of three you will be in a room, sitting at a table with your Council of Elders. One. Two. Three. You are there now. What do you see?

Unlike for Source, where I allow the client to visualize their personal concept of Source, I find that it's helpful to provide the context of how the client views their Council of Elders. I found that if I don't have the client meet with their elders in a more structured setting, the client can become easily confused and disoriented with how their elders chose to present their energies. One client experienced their elders as the wind and as you can imagine, that was both difficult for the client and I as we tried to pin down their energies to connect.

Client B: Marble floors. Marble walls. There's a table in a "V" shape and I'm sitting in front of it. There are figures looking at me.

Aliya: How many are there?

Client B: I want to say six or seven.

Aliya: What do they look like?

Client B: I can't see their faces.

Aliya: What do they have on?

Client B: Robes.

Aliya: Why can't you see their faces?

Client B: They're just looking at me and their fingers... They're holding their hands like this (the client held her hands in a steepled motion in the front of her chest). But I can tell there's six on each side. No. Three and three, and then in the middle, there's one, and that one's an older woman.

Aliya: Okay.

Client B: That's all I can tell.

Aliya: Ask them what was the purpose of that life you just led? You just saw.

Client B: What was the purpose?

A moment later...

Aliya: Are they answering you?

Client B: They're not really talking, but I've got the sense of, "To see the love."

Aliya: Oh, okay. Ask them if they have any advice for you, as you continue on your journey.

Client B: Do you have any advice for me as I continue my journey? *Be careful. Be safe. The path is open.*

Aliya: Tell them, thank you.

Client B: Thank you.

Aliya: We are going to now leave this space.

Most times the Council of Elders do not provide a wealth of information regarding the past life, but they are good for determining the purpose. What I find most interesting about visiting the Council of Elders, is the client will state that their "humanness" is recognized by the spiritual beings. Meaning, the elders are aware that it is the client's current life's energy and not the client's past life energy that is sitting before them. The elders will sometimes be tickled or annoyed by what is happening.

While we could've asked Source these questions and received the same answers, I enjoy having the client experience this spiritual connection with these spiritual beings to help the client better understand the review process after each life. Sometimes, the client will remark on a special connection (described as a friend or someone they know) with one or all of the members of their Council of Elders.

We're going to continue forward, moving forward through time and space to the Akashic Records.

If the client has a specific past life they want to view, and we plan to spend a considerable amount of time there (close to an hour), I'll guide them to that life specifically. If the client has more than one life they want to view, then we view these through the Akashic Records and spend roughly fifteen minutes exploring each. The decision to visit a full life or three to four short lives is dependent on what the client is wanting to get out of our session.

The Akashic Records are often described as a cosmic library or a vast, energetic database that holds the imprints of every soul's journey—past, present, and future. Imagine it as a spiritual diary that contains the story of the client's soul's life, including all of the soul's experiences, lessons, emotions, and wisdom gained across time.

The client's Akashic Record is a tool that can help them understand deeper patterns in their life and offer insights into why the client faces certain challenges, reveal the client's gifts or talents, and their soul's purpose. Accessing these records—often through meditation, prayer, or guided visualization—can provide clarity and support as the client navigates their path.

The term "Akashic" comes from the Sanskrit word "Akasha," meaning space or ether, which hints at the idea that these records exist beyond the physical world as part of a universal, non-physical energy field. This means that when the client taps into their Akashic Records, they're connecting with a source of knowledge that transcends time and space.

Ultimately, the purpose of taking the client to the Akashic Records is to offer guidance. Whether the client is looking to resolve recurring issues, understand their life's lessons, or simply find reassurance that they're on the right path, the records can serve as a supportive resource. The records remind the client that every experience, no matter how challenging, is part of a larger tapestry of growth and evolution, and that their journey is filled with potential and promise.

In essence, the Akashic records invites the client to explore the deeper layers of their being, encouraging them to learn, heal, and transform as they continue their spiritual path.

There are rules as we visit the Akashic Records. We cannot look at anyone else's records but our own and we must understand that the knowledge we seek must be for the good of all and cause harm to none. On the count of three, you will find yourself standing in front of the Akashic Records Library. One. Two. Three. You are now standing in front of the Akashic Records Library. Tell me, what do you see in this space?

The rules first came to me after I'd done a past life regression on my mother. My mother, like me, is connected to the Akashic Records, but unlike me, she doesn't feel welcome there and it scares her. When I'd taken her, The Keeper (one of the guides who help people access the Akashic Records) got upset and kicked her out (YouTube: @TheSpiritualGirlie, Past Life Regression 14-AUG-2024).

I knew The Keeper was upset with me for bringing her, but I still, to this day, do not know why. Before my mother, I'd taken other clients to the Akashic Records without repercussions and without stating the rules, so I was confused as to why she wasn't welcomed.

A few days after my mother's session, I felt The Keeper's energy knocking at my energetic boundary. I knew I was in trouble, so I ignored the call for a few days more, until finally, he was (what felt like) in my face, yelling at me one night.

It wasn't strange that The Keeper was yelling at me, but it was strange (to me) that I was laughing and not taking him seriously. He told me that I wasn't allowed to bring just anyone to the Akashic Records and there were rules that needed to be followed. He gave me the two simple rules noted above. It was also during this meeting that he tethered me energetically to the Akashic Records so I could have an easy way to return home...but that's for another book.

91

Client B: I see tall bookshelves. I see candles. Tall glass windows.

Aliya: Is anyone else here with you?

Client B: You and me.

There are times where the client is able to see me in astral project form with them, but this hasn't occurred often. Being able to see me in the spiritual realm provides me with confirmation of my ability to astral project, so, of course I get very excited when the client verbalizes that they can see me.

Aliya: Okay. I want you to grab your book and sit down at an empty table in the library, so we can look into your book and explore your records. Does a book stand out to you?

Client B: Yes.

Aliya: Grab your book and sit down at a table.

Client B: Okay.

Aliya: What does your book look like?

Client B: It's large and then it says my full name, the year I was born, and it's faded.

Aliya: Does it feel old or new?

Client B: Old.

Aliya: Does it have a lot of pages?

Client B: Yes. It's like about half an inch and an inch (one-and-a-half inches) thick.

Aliya: Okay, open the book and turn to the last page. You will see a number on the last page. Tell me what that number says.

Client B: Nine

Aliya: Is that the only number there?

Client B: Yeah.

Usually, the last page of the book is the last life recorded with the number there being the number of lives lived. Each page also usually holds 1 complete life portal. So, if the book is as thick as she'd described, she has lived well more than nine lives, considering that each page in the one-and-a-half-inch book is a life.

Aliya: Now, turn the book to the very first page. This is your very first life. What do you see on that page?

Client B: I see letters. I just see letters.

Aliya: What do the letters say?

Client B: I can't really make it out.

Aliya: We're going to give you healing energy in your brain, unlocking the knowledge that you know and unlocking the languages that you know. On the count of three, you will know what the letters say and be able to read your book. One. Two. Three. What does it say?

Client B: Chapter one.

Aliya: Okay. Turn the page. What is there?

Client B: I see letters, and then it's turning, and then there's, like a picture. But I can't   quite make it out. There's a picture taking up both pages.

Aliya: Okay, rub your eyes and blink. Now you'll be able to see.

The instructions are for the client to perform in the vision, not in the 3D. The client instinctively knows this as they are fully immersed in the spirit realm.

Client B: It looks like... There's a picture of a pond.

Aliya: Step into the picture on the count of three. One. Two. Three. You are now there. What do you see?

While most clients have an Akashic Records book, I've only come across two people who do not. What fascinates me is that these two people are very close to me. My mother's past lives are presented as either a wall of television screens or a very long hallway with a multitude of doors that each lead into a different past life. My daughter's past lives are displayed as thousands of orbs attached to three tall walls.

Whether the past lives are in book form or not, the clients access them the same, they have to "fall into" it. Of course, telling a client to fall into the page of a book, television screen or orb, can sometimes illicit panic as their human brain is struggling to comprehend how to fall into something like that. But I do my best to try to help them ignore logic and trust that they can lean forward energetically and tumble into the scene.

Client B: I heard crickets and grasshoppers. I see a clear sky, some clouds. It's the middle of the day.

Aliya: Look down at your body and tell me what you see.

Client B: Oh. I see… I want to say feet, but I don't see feet. I'm not sure.

Aliya: Probably not going to see feet.

Intuitively I felt she wasn't human because her energy had changed. I can't explain it and I'm not going to try to here. it was just a feeling that I had.

Client B: Yeah.

Aliya: Can you see your body to make out what you might be?

Client B: I feel like it's an animal, but it's like, morphing into different things. First, I was a big bird, maybe a flamingo.

It's very common for the soul's first life to be an animal or even an inanimate object. This always amuses the client, and they describe themselves as fully aware that they're a soul, experiencing life as an animal. Meaning, they are wholly aware of their consciousness!

As a past life regressionist, I've learned to treat all animals as if they're fully conscious of their being for fear that the bug crawling across my windshield is an aware soul visiting Earth as a bee. You'll be able to read more about why the soul choses this in Client D's session.

Aliya: Okay.

Client B: Can't really tell.

Aliya: That was your first life. We all have to get our feet wet sometimes. On the count of three, we're going to be back in the Akashic Records. One. Two. Three. You are back sitting in front of your book, are you there?

Client B: Yes.

The client had already begun to show obvious signs of fatigue such as yawning but had started to become more visibly uncomfortable by stretching and displaying facial grimaces.

Aliya: Okay. You are getting tired. So, what we're going to do, is we're going to put the book back in its place. Be very respectful of the library as we put the book back in its place.

Client B: I'm making my way to the shelf. Alright, now it's there.

Aliya: Okay, good. Our time here is at an end...

We ended the session in total awe of everything that we'd experienced during our time together. While Client B was only able to see a small piece of a past life, what she experienced instead was far more valuable. Not only was she able to meet her spirit friend and Spirit Guide, she'd also received guidance from Source and had her spiritual gifts unlocked (which was the main reason for her seeking a session with me).

After this session, I was still not aware that Noatok was connected to me. I'd assumed he was Client B's Spirit Guide and connected to her. I remember calling my mother to tell her about the unexpected visitor who'd shown up to help the client connect to her spiritual family. While having this spirit little boy "pop" in during a session wasn't the weirdest encounter I'd had since my spiritual awakening, it definitely was exciting. Just as I had after Client A's session, I left this session with Noatok feeling rejuvenated, happy, giddy and blissfully unaware that a little soul baby was mischievously inserting himself into my life.

Chapter Eight
CLIENT C
Past Life Regression: 25-AUG-2024

In June of 2024, a young woman from South Africa posted in the spiritual group that she was in the process of expanding her practice to include intuitive psychic readings and asked for volunteers (for a free psychic reading). I have been interested in psychics and tarot cards readers since I was in my early twenties and since then, I'd gone to many. I was intent on getting glimpses of my elusive my future.

I'm saying all that to say, Client C is hands down, the most genuine and skilled psychic that I'd ever had the fortune to come by. I am extremely fortunate to have been read by her.

A few months later, I'd put out a call for past life regression volunteers in the same spiritual group. Her motivations for volunteering were because she'd wanted to view a life that was most connected to the spiritual work she was doing in the 3D world. She'd also wanted to know why she felt pulled to nature. After discussing her fears of being hypnotized (I'd explained that I would put her in a trance-like state where she'd have complete control of her mind and body) and alleviating her worries by explaining what a trance was, we relaxed with some deep breathing exercises then eased into our session.

Aliya: Tell me, what do you see in this new space?

Client C: Lot's of nature. Like a forest.

Aliya: You said, *lot's of nature in the forest?*

Client C: (I'm) Out in nature in what looks like a forest, but not quite. A wilderness.

Aliya: A wilderness? Okay. What makes it look like a wilderness? Explain what that is.

Client C: There's…<inaudible>

Aliya: Can you adjust your microphone?

As I've relayed to Client C before the session, clients are able to adjust their body position, scratch their face, etc. while in the trance. To the reader it may seem here that the client is not fully in a trance, but I can assure you she was. It's important to me that the client knows they are still in complete control.

Client C: Is that better?

Aliya: That's better. What was the last thing you said?

Client C: A bear, a place where you would find, like a bear. It's a place like that. There's water. It's like walking on a mountain. It's not really mountainous per se, but it's like a rocky place.

Aliya: Oh, okay.

Client C: There's water. Like a place you would expect to go fishing.

Aliya: How do you feel being in this place?

Client C: *Hmm.* I think fine…

Aliya: Can you look at your body?

Client C: Yes.

Aliya: What do you see?

Client C: So, it's not very clear. But the clothing, I would say, it's very native, kind of native. How can I say? Almost Native American, but not quite. But that's the sense I'm getting.

Aliya: What about your hands? What do your hands look like?

Client C: Can't see anything. I can't see them.

Aliya: You can't see your hands?

Client C: No. I can really just only see my feet.

Aliya: What do your feet look like?

Client C: I'm not wearing shoes. I'm actually also on like this rocky surface, if I can put it that way. There's a bit of water there, so I could feel the water like, or see the water rather, on my feet, and I'm just kind of getting a sense of my feet, my legs, and this round thing that I'm wearing like, I'm saying very natively. It's almost like hide. Some kind of hide.

Aliya: Are your feet big or small?

Client C: Small, female size.

Aliya: They're female. Okay. What color are they?

I don't ask for color to determine the race of the past life we're viewing. I ask to help determine what type of being the client is experiencing. The spiritual realm extends deeper than race, which is a construct that this Earthly plane is built on. The client can have past lives where they are blue, purple, green, translucent, etc.

Client C: *Hmm...* They're brown.

Aliya: Brown? Okay. Is there anyone there with you?

Client C: No.

Aliya: What are you meant to do in this space?

Client C: I feel like I've wandered off from like, it's almost...how can I say? That's what I feel.

Aliya: You feel like you—

Client C: We're out. It's like we're out. I'm with other people. They're just not with me in this place, because I've wandered off to the water. It's almost like we were getting food ourselves, you know, the fish that came through with the bears. Almost like that's kind of what we were doing, but I've wondered off...

Aliya: Okay.

Client C: To the water and kind of I'm alone there, immersed in the water, if I can put it that way. In the…by the rocky, that rocky surface where there's water.

Aliya: So, we're getting our bearings in this life. What we're gonna do, is we're just going to move a little bit further, move further, further in time, to see where you live. On the count of three, we are going to be outside of your residence. One. Two. Three. You are now outside of your residence. What do you see?

Client C: Okay, yeah. So even though earlier, I said, not native American? That's kind of the sense that I'm getting, because the first thing that I heard and actually saw, but was quite quickly, so there's like, a teepee. There's like, a village of people here. Like a community, if I can put it that way. Kind of sensing and seeing and yes, it's like a teepee type of setup.

Aliya: Is that your teepee?

Client C: Oh, interesting! I didn't actually see my place. I just saw the whole village, if I can put it that way.

Aliya: Okay, okay, so let us go to your teepee. We are now inside of where you live. What do you see inside that place?

Client C: *Hmm!* So, the first thing that came through was herbs, but not any old herbs. It's almost like I don't know… It's holistic, almost like cleansing herbs like, almost like a… Yeah, it's like a <inaudible>. Enough to say that, you know, like, almost like…

Aliya: Maybe herbs for healing?

Client C: No, no, like herbs to… It's like cleansing herbs, like to cleanse the space. It's like when you're doing some kind of work, like spiritual work. So, it's almost something to cleanse the space like you know, like these sticks like you hold with like herbs, and sometimes they…

Aliya: Okay.

Client C: Sometimes they have like, sage. But this isn't sage. It's like, I don't know. It's a soft type of herb. I don't even know what that is, but that's the first thing that I'm seeing.

I could have asked for Source healing so that she could recognize the herb name and purpose, but obtaining that information wasn't beneficial at this point of the regression.

Aliya: Where do you see herbs?

Client C: Actually, I don't know. It just flashed on. It just flashed. So yeah, it's definitely inside, but I would say…on some kind of surface closer to the ground, but it's not directly on the ground. It's like, on a surface.

Aliya: Are we inside your place of residence now?

Client C: Yeah.

Aliya: What does it look like?

Client C: I'm not getting experience apart from… Yeah, I'm not getting extra sense. But I'm getting…a… I'm getting a sense that it's very minimalistic.

Aliya: Okay.

Client C: Yeah.

Aliya: Okay, do you—

Client C: Also, I'm seeing like, some kind of animal hide on the ground. Oh… Yeah, I'm not getting a sense of what that animal is, but there's definitely hide on the ground.

Aliya: The hide on the ground, is it just decoration, or do you sleep there?

Client C: <inaudible> Yes. They're known as functional. Everything has… So, this isn't in the house, but I keep on getting an eagle.

Aliya: An eagle?

Client C: Yeah, like an…an eagle with like, a like, the head is like… I don't know what eagle's heads are called, but of…like, the body has got black markings, but the…from the neck and the head is white. That's what keeps on flashing. Something about the eagle isn't coming up right.

An eagle can be a potent spiritual representation of insight, freedom and the ability to rise above earthly concerns to see the bigger picture. In a past life regression, seeing an eagle—with these specific markings—can be interpreted as a message from the client's subconscious or from a higher energetic being. White is typically associated with purity, clarity, and divine connection, and can indicate a higher, more spiritual aspect of the client's identity at work, guiding the client with wisdom and insight. While on the other hand, the black markings might symbolize the deep, sometimes hidden parts of the client's psyche—their shadow self. This combination implies a call for balance: embracing both the luminous aspects of the client's spirit and the parts that require healing or integration.

In essence, this vision may be encouraging the client to trust in her inner guidance, to honor the lessons from both light and shadow, and to embrace a journey of transformation that brings unity between all aspects of the self. While the exact meaning can be personal and unique to each individual, the eagle could've served as a powerful reminder that the client is supported by a higher perspective, capable of transcending limitations, and invited to explore the full depth of their spiritual path.

Aliya: Okay, wow, you're getting a lot of information.
Client C: Excuse me? Hello?

We experienced audio difficulties. Our computers froze for about three to five minutes. In the effort to reconnect, I'd forgotten about her mention of seeing an eagle and hadn't followed up on it. I suspect there was something there that we should have investigated, but the opportunity was missed.

Aliya: I was saying that they're giving you a lot of information at once. What we're going to do, is we're going to flash forward to dinner. To see who you are eating dinner with or taking meals with. On the count of three, you will be there. One. Two. Three.

Client C: Around an open fireplace. Again, it feels like the way dinners are held here are very community based. So, it's with the entire village around different fireplaces, but definitely around the fireplaces, with a few people surrounding it and eating over the open fire. So like, how can I say? Yeah, eating over the open fires. Almost like the food has been cooked directly over the open fire. All the sticks and things like that.

Aliya: Take a look around. Do you see a mate there?

Client C: No. But I do see a child.

Aliya: You see a child?

Client C: Yeah.

Aliya: Is it your child?

Client C: <laughter> Yeah. A boy.

Aliya: Okay, and how old is this boy?

Client C: <inaudible>

Aliya: How old? I didn't hear the number.

Client C: Six. Around, six.

This is where Noatok enters our session. I'm still not aware that I have a spiritual being connected to me or that he's showing up in my psychic reading and past life regressions.

Aliya: And how old are you?

Client C: I have to say, yeah, I feel... When I saw that boy... <inaudible>. That boy feels very Amazonian, everything about that boy says, I'm a boy who lives in the Amazon.

Aliya: Okay.

Client C: Somehow, he just feels a little bit out of place, but he's there.

Because Client C, like myself, is also curious about him, I know that we need to spend more time on his presence and what that means for my client in the current life we are viewing.

Aliya: Does he not look like everyone else?

Client C: Yeah, so, I mean, there are similarities. But yeah, I think the way he's dressed and the beads around his neck, and very rainforest-y Amazon type of look about this boy.

Aliya: Okay, so, not the same as everyone else?

Client C: Yeah. Very, yeah, like, he's dressed differently from everyone else.

Aliya: Okay.

Client C: Like, almost like, the people here are dressed in hides and kind of, you know, very Native American, if I can put it that way. The boy, he's almost just... He's not really wearing *anything* except, like, something to cover his lower part, half of the body, and then he's got his beads. And yeah...

I'm also becoming curious as to, one, how Client C (from South Africa) would know the difference, by sight, between a Native American and an Amazonian, and two, how did an Amazonian child get to America to be with a Native American tribe?

Aliya: What is he doing?

Client C: He's just laughing. Acting like he's a naughty boy. He's just laughing, like he's just, you know, like the child who's eating and enjoying themselves and just laughing and having fun. Really just giggling away.

Aliya: What is his name?

Chapter Nine

Client C: I don't know. Well, the first thing that came through was Acturu.

Not Noatok, Noah or John. So, at this point for me, there still isn't a connection to the little boy from the previous two sessions. I admit that my ego deflated a little because just for a minute, I'd wanted to believe there was a magical little boy hopping around the spiritual realm helping clients through past life regressions.

Aliya: Acturu? Okay. What is your name?

Client C: I don't know. I'm not getting a sense of that.

Aliya: You will remember your name at the count of three. You will hear someone say your name. One. Two. Three.

Client C: In Rosa.

Aliya: An Rosa?

Client C: Simosa.

Aliya: And how old are you?

Client C: I'm thirty-five.

Aliya: Now, we are going to fast forward, to what you do for work or what is your job or your responsibility in this life. On the count of three, we will be shown that. One. Two. Three. What do you see?

Client C: Yeah, I did some magic work. That's why the herbs are there.

Aliya: Okay.

Client C: That's also why I was by the water. I work with water.

Aliya: What do you do with water?

Client C: Get information. And also, from... Yeah, I get information from the water. And it's just also a good place where I go to connect very deeply. So, it's like... Go there to connect and almost like meditate, if I can say so, even though it's not anything to meditate. But that space of the water does that and (I) get information from it and healing, (and I perform) like, cleansing rituals.

Aliya: Do you get a sense of how you do that? How you work with water and get answers from water in this life?

Client C: Yeah, <inaudible>. And I've just always known what to do, how to do it, and the answers.

Aliya: We are going to move forward. We want to see a time when you are doing this, when you are connecting with water and getting answers from water. On the count of three, we will be watching you practice that. One. Two. Three. What do you see?

Client C: I'm just seeing a vastness of water almost like... Also, maybe by the...like, on a beach front, if I can put it that way. But there's a vastness of water ahead of me that I'm in the water and I'm facing away from the beach towards the vastness of water, and I just have my hands up. I don't quite know what I'm doing, but I just have my hands up, and I am speaking.

Aliya: What are you saying?

Client C: Something... So, there's a connection as I'm doing this. There's a connection that I'm calling in between the heavens and the Earth. There's an energetic meeting between below and above that is happening within the water space. What I'm saying, I haven't... Well, what am I saying?

Aliya: We're sending healing energy and Source energy to your mind to unlock the part, the language part. This is a language you know and understand very well. On the count of three, those will be unlocked so that you can hear what she is saying and relay it. One. Two. Three. What is she saying?

Client C: *Oh, God help me, for I'm praying! God help me! I'm praying!* That's what I got.

Aliya: Okay.

Client C: I feel there's more. But I just need a bit of time.

Aliya: Oh, you're fine.

Client C: And then, I call the memory within the water, almost like sacred memory that is housed in the water. Yeah, the sacred universal memory that is held within the water to come forth and to help with whatever healing. I'm trying to do this. I first call on to God, that's why I had raised up my hands, and then I call to the water directly and call on the, the, the sacred memory from the water directly that is needed. So yeah, this is definitely feeling like I work with water.

Aliya: The sacred memory that you're calling on, is it a memory of yours or is it a memory of the water?

Client C: No. It's a universal memory that is held *within* water. What I'm getting is water is holding universal memory, not so… Oh, okay, interesting. It's holding memory of that space, but it also holds universal memory. I would, I would say more of Earth and universal memory. So, it's almost like a memory of Earth, almost held from time.

Aliya: Okay, you know, yeah.

Client C: From all time, if I can put it that way. It is held within the water, right? So, it's holding that memory. That's what I'm calling upon. It is that sacred memory within Earth directly. But there's also universal, what can I say? Memory. That the water holds and that is really what I'm pulling upon.

But when I said, *interesting*, it's almost like I'm getting that and obviously of that space, right. And it's also holding memory. When I say that space, is even all of … How can I say? Healing memory from the different times and people, that go into the water and is held within the water, so as people speak, and as you know, so all of that is held in the water. Even the memories of the tribes or the people that resided there, and their rituals and their sacred practices that were practiced within the water as they were spoken within the water, and the vicinity of the water, is held in the water.

Aliya: That makes sense, because we do intentions with water. We speak to water, and it changes the property of water. So, it would make sense that such a vast body of water would hold everything. Perfect sense. Is there anything else that you want to learn from this scene?

Client C: Yeah, so, my connection. I'm just gonna say that sometimes, now I get blurred away... That this is what I just know, what I'm getting here. But what I'm getting is this, my connection with water, extends lifetimes. It is even in *this* lifetime, right. And (what) I'm getting is, directly with water, the spirit of the water, not the spirit that lives *in* water. But the spirit of the water is really what I'm getting. The *how* is still blurry.

Aliya: That's a very powerful gift she has there, or you have there, to be able to call upon the healing energy of water like that. Okay, so are you a healer in your village?

Client C: Yes, I do believe I am.

Aliya: Okay.

Client C: But I suppose, I'm a bit, I'm not... I'll say, I do feel... No, actually, no. So, I'm not getting a sense like I'm a healer where... I'm just getting that this is instinctive. Oh, I don't know how to explain that like it's not... <inaudible> everyone does this.

Aliya: Everyone does? I'm thinking it's, it's what your people do. It's your connection?

Client C: Yeah, but I actually think so for me, what I'm getting a sense of, is... Can I give you an analogy and maybe this will make sense? I don't know if you've ever watched... I feel like I'm that little girl in the water tribe. If you've ever watched like, the...

Aliya: Oh, yes!

Client C: The Last Airbender. So, yes. There would be people who do the healing work, whatever and then there's just me, right? And I get... I'm like, her in the sense that I'm not, like a prominent hero or whatever, but I am definitely someone with the gifts. But the difference with me, is almost like I'm teaching myself. I'm not learning from anyone. I'm just doing things instinctively, and it is happening. I am self-teaching. So, it's different from...

It's different a little bit from the other people who do this kind of work, in that there's, you know, you learning also from the elders, and there's all of that and then there's kind of me who's doing the things. I mean, they're still very clumsy, if I can put it that way. And this...but it's very instinctive, and it's...and it feels very...powerful, if I can put it that way. But it's just instinctive, and it's natural, and it's self-taught, like for quite a while.

I'm making the analogy of her, because I don't know, in the past. But at least that's kind of what she was doing. She was learning and discovering what she can do. Yeah, so that's kind of what I'm doing. I'm doing it very... I'm in the water very instinctively. I'm doing all of these things very instinctively and it's just kind of happening.

Aliya: Why are you self-taught? Why is no one from your tribe or your village helping you?

Client C: Oh, they can't!

Aliya: They can't?

Client C: Yeah. So, I mean, they *can*. I think the basics. But some of the stuff I'm exploring is...or some of the things... Yeah, that's all I'm getting, is they... Not that they can't. But yeah, they can't, because some of the things I am able to do through my own exploration, I really shouldn't without having gone to be trained. So, it's almost like... Oh, how do I say this? I don't know... It's almost like, actually, I don't know why, but it's almost... I'm getting the sense that, like I said, I'm feeling like I don't feel like it...

Aliya: Are you doing this in secret?

Client C: No, it's not in secret. But it's not... It's not my... It's not like my position to do so. So, like I said, I'm not like a healer. I'm not a water bender in the tribe necessarily, though, the gift is definitely there. But actually, I'm also even getting a sense that maybe people don't know that I can, that I can do the things that I can do.

Aliya: And why aren't you telling them that?

Client C: *Hmm.* Yeah, again, they can't. I'm getting a sense that I'm getting... I get... I am... Oh, I see, I am to get instructed. I don't. Actually, I don't know why I'm not telling them, but I'm getting a sense that I am to be instructed directly, if that makes sense. (I need to) Go through a mentor, right? So, (I'm getting trained) directly from Spirit, if I can put it that way. From Nature herself, from... That's how I'm getting taught. I'm also getting that most of the healers here are male.

Through this past life experience, we were able to answer one of the questions the client wanted to know. What is her connection to nature? Since she'd had a past life where Nature itself taught her how to connect, it would make sense for that knowledge to transcend across multiple lifetimes.

Aliya: Oh, okay.

Client C: I'm not male.

Aliya: That would be a reason why you're keeping it quiet?

Client C: Yeah, most of them are male. And actually, it's as though my gift, like I said, I mean, it's almost stronger.

Aliya: Okay.

Client C: That's the thing.

Aliya: You said, Nature is showing you?

Client C: Yeah.

Aliya: How does Nature talk to you and show you what to do?

Client C: I just know.

Aliya: Just know. Okay. In your life, what is your affinity towards plants?

Client C: In which life, in this life?

Aliya: Yes, in the life we're viewing.

Client C: That's not coming through. Apart from the fact that I had the herbs in my teepee, that came through.

Aliya: I'm sending you some Source healing energy right now. You're getting a lot of information. We're just sending it to you to help resolve some of the issues that are starting to crop up. Some tiredness, some sleepiness, some confusion. We're just easing all that away. How do you feel?

The client was yawning and shifting her body, as if she was uncomfortable. Sending her Source healing helped to restore and provide her with energy to finish the session.

Client C: I'm feeling fine, except I'm <inaudible> I am right now.

Aliya: You're what right now?

Client C: I'm feeling pressed like I need to go to the bathroom.

Aliya: Oh, do you have to use the bathroom?

Client C: Yes, I feel I need to use the bathroom.

Aliya: When you go the bathroom, you're just gonna release limitation, anger, or whatever. That's why you're feeling like you need to use the bathroom. When you return, you will be even more relaxed. What you're gonna do now, is you're just gonna take out your earbuds, go use the bathroom safely and then come back, and I will be right here.

Client C: Definitely.

Clients often feel the need to use the bathroom during intense healing sessions because the body and mind are deeply interconnected. Energetic healing work, like past life regressions or trauma release, often stimulates both emotional and energetic shifts. Emotional healing involves releasing pent-up energy or emotional blocks.

During emotional or energetic healing, the body may process physical detoxification as part of the release. The body's energy systems (such as the chakras) process this release, which can activate the nervous system and trigger a physical response, such as the urge to use the restroom. This response is natural and often signals that the session is working to facilitate release and transformation.

Once the client returned, it took roughly five minutes to get her back into a relaxed trance-like state. Surprisingly, the client fell back into a relaxed state fairly quickly.

Aliya: Now, we are going to fast forward to an important day in this life. A day that will give you insight of how this life connects to the current life. One. Two. Three. What do you see?

Client C: Water. I'm dressed in white.

Aliya: And what is going on in the scene?

Client C: I'm doing some kind of work with water, with full puddles of water.

Aliya: Okay. Is there anyone with you?

Client C: Yeah, there's a group of other people in the water, but I'm the one who's...

Aliya: Oh, okay.

Client C: The hands raised and doing the work with the water. Yeah.

Aliya: So, the people that are with you, are they male or female?

Client C: A combination.

Aliya: How did we get here? Because before you said just the men (could be healers) and you weren't a healer, how did we get here?

Client C: Oh, yeah, no, I... Oh, interesting. I'm not in that lifetime anymore. I'm somehow here.

Aliya: Oh, you're here?

Client C: Yeah. yeah, no, I'm not there anymore. This is a completely different... I'm here, in this lifetime.

Aliya: Okay. So, we're seeing a scene from this life? And that's, well, that's how it (the past life and present life) connects. We asked how it connects.

Client C: *Hmm.*

Aliya: So, sometime in this life, you are going to be doing water work.

Client C: The healers, those people there (with her in the scene she's viewing) are healers. I'm helping them with something.

During our debriefing, after the session, the client relayed that she saw me as one of the healers in this scene.

Aliya: Okay, okay, that makes sense. Is there anything that you want to see from this scene before we move on?

The client may be in the middle of looking at something that I can't see, or receiving spiritual downloads, so I don't want to pull them from the scene prematurely.

Client C: No.

Aliya: On the count of three, we will be back in that past life we were just viewing. One. Two. Three. What do you see?

Client C: I'm in the village.

Aliya: What are these people called?

Client C: I'm getting Tomahawk. Whatever, Tomahawk has to do with this.

Aliya: Tomahawk? Okay, that's a Native American tribe. What planet are you on?

Client C: On Earth.

Aliya: Okay, I just wanted to make sure.

Usually, once the client connects to the past life, I establish the time, place and the where (Earth, different dimension or different planet). But we hadn't done that yet, so it was good to confirm here.

Aliya: And that little boy you saw earlier, who did not quite look like everyone else. What is the significance of him being in the tribe?

I actually don't know what made me think of the little boy again, especially since we hadn't seen him since she'd returned from the restroom. But he had been on my mind, so I asked about him to close that loop.

Client C: No, so he's not… So, I'm getting a sense, that he's… This is a flash of another life, or another connection.

Aliya: Okay.

Client C: He's not actually, yeah… Like I said, he's out of place. So, he's not actually there, even though he's appearing here. But he's out of place. He doesn't… Actually, it doesn't feel to me, that he's actually part of this community. But for whatever reason, he's popping up in this space.

Aliya: So, what is he?

Client C: Yeah, Amazon. Like I'm feeling he's from the Amazon, back when he's very strong to me.

Aliya: Is he human?

Chapter Ten

Client C: Oh, yeah, he's human, like a little boy.

Aliya: *Hmm...* I'm just wondering how someone from the Amazon is in the Native American tribe?

Client C: Yeah. That's why I'm almost... It almost feels like, instead of... He's not actually... He's there, but not there. I don't know how to explain this. It's almost like a vision, if I can put it that way. Though in this setting... But you can see that he's out of place. He doesn't... Actually, it's almost like I... Only *I* can see this boy, if I can put it that way.

Aliya: Can you see him now?

Client C: Yeah, I think, yeah, I can see.

Awareness hit me. I know this little boy, but the likelihood of him showing up in two different past life regressions, one after the other gave me doubts. But even so, my curiosity was piqued. I sat up taller in my office chair and leaned closer to the laptop. Something magical and otherworldly was definitely at play here. I just didn't have a clue as to what *exactly.*

Aliya: I want you to go up to the little boy and ask him who he is to you.

Client C: So, he's telling me. Well, I'm getting <inaudible>. He's not interested in telling me about who he is to me, but I get a sense that he's my child. But what this child wants to do is to grab my hand because, he said, I need to go to the forest, and he wants to lead me into the forest.

He grabbed Client C's hand, just as he'd grabbed Client B's, to lead them someplace they needed to see. Very interesting...

Aliya: Okay, you're gonna follow him.

Client C: Yeah.

Aliya: You can let him take your hand and lead you to the forest. But I want you to continue to narrate everything that you see and what is being done and what he's saying to you. Okay? Let him lead you to the forest.

Client C: He's grabbing my hand, like I said, he's only dressed... Yeah, he's just really only covered his private parts. He's, you know, like his private parts are only covered. And he's grabbing...and we're walking. We're just walking in the forest, like there's this vastness of trees. I'm seeing... I'm seeing what looks like a, I don't know, a leopard. Not a leopard! Oh, a black animal! A jaguar.

Months after I session, in speaking with Client C about writing this book, she informed me that she'd felt that the little boy and the jaguar both had a connection to me. I know now my connection with Noatok, but will have to explore more the significance of the jaguar.

Aliya: Okay.

Client C: Somewhere there, or something like that, but it's quite far. But we're just walking, right. And it's a very lush place and it's important for me to be in that space, is all I'm getting.

Aliya: Okay.

Client C: I need to be in that space. That's why he's leading me here.

Aliya: Okay.

Client C: Amongst the trees. But again, there's a strong water, this is a rainforest, there's a water aspect that's very strong, that's coming through here.

Aliya: Okay.

Client C: And I was feeling very emotional, like when he was taking me. I could almost cry, right. The space that he's taking me to.

Aliya: Ask him what—

Client C: So, there's—

Aliya: What does this space mean to you? What space is it?

Client C: So, I'm getting that. Yeah, again, this is linked to almost that question I asked about.

Aliya: Yeah.

Client C: Something about the people here could actually communicate with the plants and hear the message and get lessons about the plants. What feels... What <inaudible>, and just a lot of ways of how to live in harmony with nature. Which they learn directly from Mother Earth, right, from nature and living with the animals and the plants and there is knowledge there. That I'm getting, that the people here, right? That I'm a part of... That come from here and know how to do this, and they communicate and understand it and there's a very strong sense of like, I'm saying, oh, just living very harmoniously with nature and understanding nature.

And there's a balance here, right? There's a way of being, and a way of balance, if I can put it that way. Which is almost a... Which is a Universal Law, if that's what's coming through. Are of sorts, right? Around balance that these people understood very well. But it is really around communication with nature and the water, and how these two come in. That these people that lived here. This feels very home.

Aliya: Okay.

Client C: You know the people who live here amongst the trees. The trees are very old and ancient, and they also hold a lot of memory. And the trees and the plants, they teach these people a lot, you know. And there's something around being in this space or to go there to be able to remember.

Aliya: Are you remembering now? Well, you are cause you just, you just said everything. <laughter>

Client C: Yeah. But I guess this is where the other side of the brain... Yeah. Okay. So, my question was, but how? And the thing is, it's not the how, it's just to let go and be, is what I'm getting.

Aliya: Oh, okay.

Client C: Yeah. And it comes within that space. When I connect and I'm just still, I can hear what I'm doing. Which is actually what happens here, but I don't know in this lifetime, in a way. I can hear, right, like, I was saying earlier. There's something there that I don't quite hear very clearly.

Aliya: Maybe just being introduced back into the space will begin to open all that up?

Client C: What I'm getting is, it's similar to what we're doing, right? Because one can travel there energetically. That's what I'm getting. You travel there energetically. The... It's not... It's the mind. That's what I'm getting.

Aliya: Okay.

Client C: That's why I don't hear very well. It's me, like, I don't know how to say that it's almost like, my mind is very busy, and there's a lot of expectation around when it comes to that. But the thing... Oh, okay, I get it now. The thing about that space is, there isn't that, right? Because of the water, the plants, the vastness of it, or you are able to just be so in the moment that you can hear. That's what I'm doing.

Aliya: Oh, okay. Do you know how to get back there on your own?

Client C: Well, yeah, I'm getting, he will always be there to guide me back, the same way he took me there.

Retrospectively, I'm wondering why my soul baby is connected to Client C and why he's telling her that he'll help to lead her back to this space?

Aliya: Okay, he will guide you back. He will always guide you. Okay. And what is his name?

Client C: *Hmm.* I'm getting, <laughter> *"I told you my name."* I don't know now. Now, I forgot... I'm not getting to do... I'm just, I just... I'm just getting that, *"I told you my name."*

Aliya: He did. I don't think I wrote it down. Is he talking to you?

Client C: No, he doesn't talk. He just smiles, and we...and just kind of holds my hand, right, and like I said, it's...

Although, this boy doesn't have the same name as Client B stated before. I'm instinctively drawn to this boy and energetically feel that he's the same boy from the day prior. Especially, once Client C confirmed that the boy does not talk. There are other similarities with the prior reading (too many to ignore), such as, smiling, laughing, grabbing the client's hand to lead the client on an adventure, and him being out of place in the life he first encountered the clients in.

Aliya: Now, I've seen him before. Can you ask him what is his connection to me?

Client C: *Hmm,* Okay. You were friends. I'm seeing a little... There's another child, I can't tell if it's a boy or girl, but that's what I'm getting, like someone... Yeah, that's what I'm getting, friends or somebody. Yeah, like kids, the same age. That played together.

Aliya: Okay, so we're friends?

Client C: Yeah, like you're friends, or yes? Well, at least definitely played together. That's for sure.

Aliya: Okay, that's for me to explore later, on my own. Tell him, thank you. We appreciate his help. Okay, is there anything else that he needs to say to you, or can we move on?

Client C: So, actually, there's clarity there. Yes, you're friends, but you're related, like cousins or something like that.

Aliya: We're related?

Client C: Yeah.

This was the first mention that I was related to this boy and confirmation that it was, in fact, my connection to him that brought him forward. I did want to explore this more, but the client was getting tired (the energy from Noatok is very heavy) and we still had another spiritual place to visit before the session ended.

Aliya: Is there anything else that he wants to show us, or can we move on?

Client C: Yeah, I'm getting. I just need to stay here for a little bit.

Aliya: Okay. We don't have a whole lot of time. So, what we're going to do, it will be a couple of minutes on this (energetic) plane, but where you are, time has no restriction. You do everything that you need to do, but will only be a couple of minutes where I am.

Although, I would like a recounting of what the client is learning and experiencing, I'm also aware of the reason for these sessions. The reason is not to satisfy my own curiosity, but to connect the client with their purpose, illuminate and heal any traumas, help them find their path and accomplish anything else needed spiritually.

I'm also aware that the client may be receiving healing and/or instruction from Source or their spiritual team that the client 1) may not be ready to remember the information provided in the 3D world or, 2) should not record the information being given and that information shouldn't be heard by me or shared with the world.

Five seconds later...

Client C: That's fine. You can continue.

Aliya: You're done?

Client C: Yes.

Aliya: Okay, good. Thank him for his time.

Client C: Thank you.

Aliya: We are now going to move to the last day of the current life you are viewing. The last day of her on the count of three. One. Two. Three. What do you see?

Client C: Firstly, there's... <inaudible>...When I went to the bathroom, I experienced stomach issues... <inaudible>... It's males, very kind of unhappy, but they're like dragging, dragging me. I'm struggling, right, like, I'm fighting, trying to fight them all. Yeah, it doesn't... Yeah, but these people actually are not happy with my gifts.

The client was experiencing obvious distress at the scene she was viewing. I had to get control of the situation and calm her down as much as I could.

Aliya: What we're gonna do, is we're going to slow down and send Source healing to your stomach and to your mind and your soul. You are just viewing this life. You cannot be harmed. It's already happened. We're just pulling information from it. Okay. Now, you can continue to... What is happening? They're dragging her?

Client C: Yeah, like, I'm saying, it's almost like, yeah, she's trying to fight them off, like, I'm trying to fight them all for dragging me. It has to do with the gifts, and like I said, it has to do with the, I guess, a master. Like, I've mastered.... It's where I am, gift-wise, is at a master's level. And something about that is making the people in this community, the males in this community, very unhappy, I mean? I'm not... I don't know, but the point is, there's a dragging and a persecution of sorts, that's happening there.

Aliya: And how old are you?

Client C: I'm still the same.

Aliya: You're still the same? Oh, okay.

Client C: Yeah. so relatively young. Yeah.

Aliya: Okay.

Client C: Thirty-five. Thirty, late thirties.

Aliya: Now, you are about to take your last breath in this life. Your soul is about to leave this body. On the count of three, we will see the soul ascend. One. Two. Three. What do you see?

Client C: Oh! Yeah, as I'm ascending this life <inaudible>.

Aliya: It's what?

Client C: Are you asking me? What am I seeing as I ascend this lifetime?

Aliya: Yes, as the soul leaves the body.

Client C: Yeah, so definitely that day, as I was being dragged, I was killed.

Aliya: Okay.

Client C: As part of this whole dragging. And... and... Yeah.

Aliya: What is the soul doing as it leaves the body?

Client C: Just observing.

Aliya: Does it stay awhile?

Client C: I'm observing. Yeah, I'm observing the hanged body.

Aliya: Oh, they hung her?

Client C: Yeah.

Aliya: Do you stick around, or do you start to leave?

Client C: Stick around.

Some souls stay for a few minutes and watch as their body is mourned and some leave almost immediately.

A few minutes later...

Aliya: Are you leaving now?

Client C: Yeah.

Aliya: Okay.

Client C: Yeah, actually, I...I can't even see the body, partly.

Aliya: Okay.

Client C: <inaudible>

Aliya: We are thanking that life for letting us view it and for giving us insight. We are leaving and we are moving through time and space and energy. At the count of three, you will be in front of Source and the presence of Source. One. Two. Three. What do you see?

Client C: <laughter> It's funny. Oh, gosh! How do you even say this? I see a... I see Morgan Freeman. I don't know.

Aliya: <laughter> Morgan Freeman?

Client C: I don't know. That's... but the point is, I just see a male with white hair. And yeah, it looks like Morgan Freeman.

I made an executive decision here to reimagine Source as I didn't want us to get distracted by talking with "Morgan Freeman".

Aliya: One second. Okay, we're gonna try this again. So, now that we've looked back at the life we just came from, what I want you to do now, is you're going to move forward and we're going to be introduced to Source. On the count of three, you will find yourself in the direct presence of Source. One. Two. Three. You are now present with Source. Tell me, do you feel the energy of Source present in this new space?

Client C: It's just the vastness, that's all I feel.

Aliya: Okay, do you see what's in the vastness?

Client C: I cannot explain that. It's almost like, it's just... It's just like a... both light and dark.

Aliya: Okay.

Client C: It's like, it's like darkness, but there's a light about it. I don't know.

Aliya: Okay.

Client C: Yeah, yeah.

Aliya: How does it feel?

Client C: Obviously calm. So, there's definitely a vastness about it. But there's a calmness about it.

Aliya: Okay.

Client C: ...About this feeling.

Aliya: Do you recognize the feeling?

Client C: Yes.

Aliya: We are going to ask Source our questions. Source, are there any blockages that <Client C> has that's impeding her in this life?

I'm going to point out here that I am very respectful of Source and am in awe of its infinite power. When I present to Source, I make sure to ask Source if we can ask questions, but I'm noticing here that I hadn't done that. This oversight is purely on my part, of course, but I also want to acknowledge this oversight, even if after the fact.

Client C: What I'm told is the feelings that I, the things, the sensations, it has to do with the sensations I was feeling at the beginning which was within my heart, and I would say...and the sacral. It's really around the healing work within those areas, right? Cause that's what's been impacted and I'm getting that I... I'll submit contracts. I can say that they're karmic contracts in which some of that power was given away.

Aliya: Oh!

Client C: Which is residing in those areas, right? Due to some of the experiences. And... yeah, and I know, right, it's in some of the relationships and then there's just other...there's stuff. There's also some that I'm getting. So, what I'm getting, I'm just, I'm just really repeating it like, what I know, and I guess it's the confidence, right? Yes, there's also...there's that aspect, right? Due to the past. But then there's also aspects in which like, I would say, energy is directed towards me. Because, before my own awakening, or it's like, it's like I can say, my light was shining...

Aliya: Okay.

Client C: And there were things about me that people could see that I couldn't see. There's a lot of energy that's directed towards me to try to take that, like, for themselves. Yeah.

Aliya: Oh, okay.

Client C: So, there's... And I think that it's just a matter of... Yeah. And again, yeah, you not to give that stuff attention. And really <inaudible>.

Aliya: What did you say last? What was the last part?

Client C: It's just an awareness for me to be... It's just for me to be... Not to give it too much energy, but to be aware. This is confirmation of actually something I heard earlier today. But it's just to be aware that this is happening, that there is active spell work happening. But...and just also for me to, just be in my awareness, take my own protective measures, if I can put it that way. Okay, yeah, just being aware of it.

Aliya: Can we release any of those blockages today?

Client C: Yes. What I'm getting is the fact that I even think I have blockages is part of the problem, right? So, yes. The only thing that I'm getting is really just to kind of be aware of my thoughts and to read, because that is quite powerful, and that in itself can create the manifestation and cause permeability.

Aliya: Okay.

Client C: Yeah. within my own energetic field.

Aliya: Now, how can we strengthen... Can we strengthen your energetic field today and protect your energetic field today?

Client C: Yeah. So, what I'm getting is, yes, and it all comes from within myself in the sense that, when I... I just need to focus on my authentic self and doing the things that is hard led, right? And really listening to that <inaudible> and nothing else. And where there is... Where there are things that come up, or that shows that there's a feeling, or there's wound and just to really give that attention and just move on. But the gist of all of this is really not to focus my attention outwardly, is to focus within myself and focus within that sensitivity that I was getting within that solar plexus.

The more I get to know myself, and the more I just trust that, and to be authentic, and be as I'm led from within. The more I am able to stand in my power, and when I stand in my power. Yeah, that's, yeah. Okay. So, I'm very protected as it is. But the more I stand within my power, there really isn't much that anything anyone can do. It's really... The gist of it is really, it's really me, right? And focusing within and getting to know myself and standing within my power and focusing only really on that.

Aliya: Okay.

Client C: That's what I'm getting.

Aliya: I get that. Okay. We're asking Source, what is the star seed connection that you have with Sirius and Acturian?

Chapter Eleven

Client C: I'm asked not to, necessarily, not to elaborate, but it is exactly as I got it in my dream last night, and as I interpreted it. So that's the confirmation I'm getting.

Aliya: Okay, it's telling you not to elaborate? It's just telling you that?

Client C: It's exactly as I interpreted it in my dream.

Aliya: Okay. Okay.

It felt as though Source wanted this information to be private without my knowledge. I also got a vision that Source did not want the information he provided to the client to be disseminated to the general public. At the time of this session, the thought of publishing the session tapes was not on my mind, let alone writing this book. But, despite this, I saw that Source didn't want this information to be published and known publicly so I didn't push the topic.

Aliya: What are your gifts?

Client C: So yeah, so I don't know how else to explain this except the way it was explained to me.

Aliya: Yes, that's good.

Client C: I used to have a need to... This thing that was pulling me towards a certain healer in South Africa here before they passed away and I really didn't know anything about this work. But anyways, the point is that it's almost a high. How can I say? He was really big, but for lack of a better word, I'll say a high priest, or I have... So, confirmation of the ones that I do know is I'm able to get information and to all source senses, and they're all not even strong. But they're all quite strong, right? Through all the various source senses. Then there's definitely the dreams. Which is the other aspect of it. The part of dreams is on two aspects. There's the one where it's for knowing and information and there's one for seeing, almost prophetic. If I could say, seeing into.

Aliya: Okay.

Client C: You know, if that makes sense?

Aliya: Yes, it does.

Client C: So, there's that, and then there's the water, right? Oh, there's something called... I don't know what's this word... There are people who pray, right? And so basically is, I guess, speaking into water, as well. Yeah, right. And so that one thing... So, it's like praying into water, and through that, that frequency is in the water. And that's what I heard. And then, there's the hands that I was asking about. But this is, really this is, around energy work. This is energy work.

Aliya: Okay, energy work. Okay. Asking Source, what does <Client C> need to do to activate these gifts, if they're not already activated?

Client C: *Hmm.* Yeah, so I'm getting... There really are, but it's more on following my guidance. I get guidance both specific places and when I get that, so the first thing that came up is patience. That's the first thing and the other one was to really follow your guidance. So, when I get strong urges to go to specific places, is to go to these places, right? You don't need to know when, why or how. But there is something about the places that is activated.

Aliya: Okay.

Client C: And also, just following the guidance, sometimes it is to listen to specific... Oh, readers, yeah. Sometimes this is, like, sometimes these readers and messages that come through to that specifically. But then there's also around certain books and courses that I'm always directed to, that I always just start and never finish, so it is to really to persevere, not to take on too much. But when we start one thing, to see it through.

Yeah, that's the biggest thing. So, what I'm getting is, I get a lot of information at one time and what I need to learn to do, right, is to…it's sort of not the right word, but yeah, to kind of <inaudible>. Yeah, that's a better word. Which one is the one that I need to focus on now and then do that and see that through. Instead of taking it all on, and then kind of just leaving them all, that sort of thing.

Aliya: I get what you mean. Okay. What is your soul's name?

Client C: Well, the first thing that came through is Samson.

Aliya: Samson? Okay.

Personally, I believe knowing your soul's name is a powerful revelation. By giving your soul an identity other than the physical body (which it isn't), you're able to wake up fully and begin embracing who you really are—a divine being. Discovering your soul's name is a profound step on the path of spiritual awakening. It is more than just a name—it is a vibrational essence, a sacred key that unlocks deeper layers of your soul's purpose, wisdom, and truth. When you connect with your soul's name, you align with your Higher Self and the unique energy signature that defines your eternal being.

Spiritually, learning your soul's name fosters a sense of divine connection and self-empowerment. It can dissolve feelings of separation and remind you of your eternal bond to Source. By speaking or meditating upon your soul's name, you activate a portal to greater self-awareness and inner peace, allowing you to live more authentically and in alignment with your highest purpose.

The impact of this revelation ripples through your life— strengthening your intuition, deepening your spiritual practice, and anchoring you in the truth of who you are. It becomes a guiding light, reminding you of your sacred journey and helping you navigate challenges with clarity and grace. Learning your soul's name is not just an act of discovery, but a sacred homecoming to your truest self.

Aliya: Asking Source, how can \<Client C> pull back fragments of her soul and energy to herself?

Client C: Yeah, it's exactly the same answer that we got before. It's not around focusing externally really to get... So, even when information is coming externally, it's not to say go to that person to view this. There is just a little message in there for me about things that I... So, I'm getting that I can actually do all these things myself, right?

Aliya: Okay.

Client C: And to really look within myself, and to really see what is resonating. A lot of the things that is being pointed to externally is not so much to seek help externally, but it is to help with remembering, or to point me in the direction in which I need to kind of follow. So, my thing is never to...how can I say? I think, never really to follow...what...

In all messages that I'm getting, one of my gifts is a gift of discernment, where I would hear the message, right? But I will discern to hear the truth beyond the message and not the surface level in the message. So, there's the gift of that discernment. It is really to go and either in the courses or in videos, or wherever I am guided to go, is to hear that out and to extract.

I'm almost seeing, kinda like a surgeon. Like, almost like, a surgery type of thing, right? I am able to extract, with precision, what I need to do from that message, and it is never really the way it is explained in that message. But I will know. That's what I'm doing.

Aliya: Okay. Is there any healing that needs to take place right now that Source can help you with?

Client C: Yes, So there's two things, and there's the vulnerability, right? And there's anger or rage, if I can put it that way. And the two of those together, so it is really to let go. Allow yourself to let go and to be vulnerable.

Aliya: Can Source help you with that today?

Client C: Yes.

Aliya: Okay, we're going to ask Source to help with that today. In that place, while it's taking those things that no longer serve you in this life away, in its place, we are going to inject Source healing energy. So, as Source is taking that away, in that space, we're not going to leave it empty, we're going to put in Source healing energy back in that space. How do you feel?

Client C: <inaudible>

Aliya: What did you say?

Client C: I'm saying, it's difficult to explain how I feel. I could, just so I could definitely feel a sensation happening within.

Aliya: That's it. We don't have to pick it apart or analyze it. We just let go and, right? Just let go and be, and let Source do its work and trust that it's done. Is there any secret that Source can reveal to you today?

Client C: Yeah.

Aliya: Yes? Is Source revealing them to you?

Client C: Again, confirmation.

Aliya: Okay, are you going to remember the secret?

Client C: Oh, yeah, it's just around, again, you know, everything is not all of my relationships, even close ones, and this is not conscious on my side, or anything, or in my house. It is just that I always have that awareness and discernment because of, I guess, how can I say, the work I need to do, if I can follow that.

Yeah. So, again, it links to some energy that is meant to derail in some other way... But yeah, so it is just confirmation that is around some of the relationships I had. But it is more of an awareness that I need to embody, right? But it's also not just around the awareness, right? It's also around the state in which I need to remain, never around...blame or hate or anything like that because that doesn't serve me in any way.

Aliya: Okay. Asking Source, how many lives has <Client C> lived?

Client C: Numerous, so I'm getting that.

Aliya: Numerous? Okay.

Client C: Numerous. I'm an old soul.

Aliya: Okay. That would make sense. Yeah, okay. A question for Source for myself, are there any secrets that Source can tell me today?

Client C: Similarly, you need to also be aware around your... Okay, so there's two things, that you need to be aware of again, just like, what they're teaching me around your relationships and the ones that don't serve you. But in the same way... Yes. Guard your heart, if I could put it that way, but not to close it off. Just be careful around your own frequency and when you discover these relationships, because I'm getting that you are going to, if you haven't already started discovering that.

And then, the other one is around, also, similarly, around, just vulnerability. That is coming through for you. In your own journey, that as you open up your own sense of vulnerability, is really going to strengthen your work, your gifts and just general, even in the physical, outside of your spiritual work, just in your day-to-day life. So, is to open yourself up to the color pink, if that makes sense. Which is a very soft feminine, divine feminine energy, which is attached to your heart center.

Aliya: Okay, I understand that. This is another Source question for myself, who is that little boy who'd showed up to guide you today and who'd shown up to guide my other client the other day? What is... Who is he, and what is his connection to me?

Client C: I don't know. All that's coming through is... He's part of a Heyoka. He's a Heyoka empath.

Aliya: A what?

This was my first time hearing the term, Heyoka empath. A broader explanation of a Heyoka empath is discussed at the end of this book.

Client C: There's something about this boy that is an archetypal energy. A very playful energy that allows... That's a mirroring energy. So, that's all I'm getting, right? Not necessarily around this lifetime, or what's the tangible. But there is an archetype that he is... That he embodies, right? He is a very strong empath, which is called a Heyoka empath, right? Very powerful and are really... Very... Can be... How can I say? And it's not, I'll say, trickster, but it's not a trickster in a, in the negative connotation of a trickster, but just a very strong way, a mirror. That's all that's coming through. But in terms of who he is, he embodies that energy.

Her explanation of Noatok is the same that I'd had during Client A's psychic reading. An energy of a trickster or sprite, but nothing negative. But even here, I'm sad to report that I hadn't made the connection it was him that I'd met during Client A's session.

Aliya: Okay.

Client C: Let's see if I can get anything from who he is to you. Yeah, so, all that's coming through now is in whichever lifetime or whatever, but I'm just getting, nephew.

Aliya: Okay?

Client C: So, yeah, I don't know, but I'm not getting anything other than that. But the strong, prominent thing is around the energy that this little one embodies. Which allows, very strong energy, that allows one to see themselves, and to really be in there with self.

Aliya: *Hmm*, okay. I was starting to wonder if that was one of my Spirit Guides. And in this life, it would have been my Uncle Todd.

Client C: Yeah, there's something around like I'm saying, nephew, some that kind of nephew type of relationship. So, I don't know if you, and it... I don't know. So, that's really all I'm getting. Let me ask... I don't know if I'm getting...

Aliya: Yeah, ask.

Client C: <laughter> I'm laughing, because, like again, I see this little... I just see him just again, smiling and laughing and saying, not to be lazy.

Aliya: <laughter> Oh, that's for me. I gotta figure it out. I'm trying to get all these shortcuts.

Client C: <laughter> Yes! That's why I'm checking like, stop being lazy.

As mentioned earlier, most of the transformative aspects of my life are hidden from me. I understood that Source and Noatok wanted me to uncover the truth myself, stop trying to go the easy route and to put the work and effort in to find out for myself.

Aliya: Okay, okay, I get, I get it. Does Source have anything that Source wants to tell us before we go?

Client C: Yeah. So, you and I are somehow connected. Yeah, beyond this life.

Aliya: Oh, okay, we're connected beyond this life?

Client C: Part of the same soul group is what I'm hearing. Somehow.

Aliya: Oh! Okay, we're finding... I figure I'm finding soul groups now, soul people. And so, I am trying to just connect. That's nice to hear. Well, hello, friend!

Client C: Hello!

Aliya: Okay, do you have any questions for Source before we leave?

Client C: No, I didn't, but I did hear... I see a lot. Yeah, that's what I'm just getting here. I see a lot, and it is very accurate, is what I'm getting. And just to test it.

Aliya: Okay, okay. Thank you and thank Source.

Client C: Thank you, Source. Very grateful.

Aliya: Okay, let's see, our time here is coming to an end.

As stated at the beginning of Client C's session. I'd previously connected to her during a psychic reading she'd done for me. I'd already felt a connection to her, a connection that I couldn't explain. It just felt like we were linked somehow.

What this spiritual journey has taught me, is that we're all connected to each other in some way or another, big or small. I'm particularly excited to meet and connect with other souls, but there's something...dare I say, spiritual, in finding members of your soul tribe. While life may take Client C and myself in different directions as we both follow our own distinctive spiritual paths, I'm quite certain that our energies will connect again soon.

I left this session with my head spinning. I'd sat down and tried to figure out how often this little boy had shown up in readings and regressions and if I'd missed any other sightings. This is when I'd remembered the "sprite" from Client A's reading. He had been with me for months and I hadn't known!

Satisfied that he'd only showed up with these three clients, so far, I made it a point to try to figure out "why". Had he shown up to these particular clients because of their energy and that made the connection easier? Or was it because these three clients were connected to me as part of my soul tribe? These were only some of the questions I had, but the one I needed answering right away was, "Who the heck was this little boy and why was he showing up?"

It was time to stop being lazy and figure it out.

Aliya Griffin

Chapter Twelve
Aliya
Meditation: SEP-2024

Sometime in September 2024, I decided to figure out who Noatok was to me and why he kept showing up and hijacking some of my past life regression session. As you can tell from the previous pages, it took me a short while to understand that *I* was the connection and not my clients. I was the link between Noatok and the others.

I'd found a self-guided meditation video on YouTube that would put me into a state of relaxation. Ready for bed, I settled into a comfortable position and turned on the video to begin my journey. While totally relaxed and energetically aligned with the spirit realm, I called forth Noatok's energy.

He showed up in an all-white space as the same little boy I'd seen during the intuitive psychic reading, which I knew was also the same dark haired, tanned little boy that my clients had also seen. The following is a general account of what was discussed and shown.

I recognized him immediately, feeling a deep loving connection to him. "Noatok! It's you!"

I asked him why he was showing up as a little boy and he replied, "This is how you recognize me."

"I want to see what you really look like."

Noatok changed from a little boy to a bright white light of energy. My heart filled with so much love and joy. While I'd initially recognized the little boy as Noatok, when he revealed his true energetic self, the feeling of recognition and love expanded tenfold. I was in shock and awe. His energy reminded me of my oldest son, but not quite.

I told him, "This is how I want you to show up all the time."

He laughed, but eventually changed back to the little boy.

I asked him, "Who are you to me?"

"Your son."

"How are you my son?"

"You and our father, through your love, decided to create life. You created two of us, twins, a male and female."

Immediately, I remembered my daughter (who I hadn't remembered existed until now) and I became protective and upset. "Where is my daughter?!" I glanced around the space, searching for my daughter, instantly missing her energy and presence.

(I can't remember where he said she was or if he told me, but I calmed down some and we were able to continue our conversation)

"Why are you here? Why did you come to me?"

"I heard your call for help and came to help."

He'd also explained that he was helping me now and I'd had a vision of him holding out his arms, holding my Spirit Guides back, telling them that he can take care of me for a while.

Unfortunately, the session wasn't recorded so I can't give a true accounting of what all was discussed after this. All I know is that I woke up hours later feeling calm, loved and watched over.

Chapter Thirteen
CLIENT D
Past Life Regression: 22-OCT-2024

In October 2024, I'd put out a call for volunteers who wanted a free past life regression. I hadn't done one for almost a month because I'd been working through my spirituality and purpose. My energy for the past month had been up and down and all over the place. I'd been looking for another job (after being released from mine a few months prior) but in reality, psychic readings and past life regressions was the only "job" I wanted.

For the first time in my life, I'd found my calling. I was both happy and sad at this revelation. Happy that I'd finally experienced what a true calling felt like and sad that I lacked the clients to make a living using my spiritual gifts.

Client D was a young South African woman with a warm and infectious bubbly personality. Aside for her predetermined questions for Source, she'd wanted to see a life with wings, if she'd had a life where she abused her power and a life most connected to her current life. I didn't expect anything out of the ordinary.

Aliya: I want you to tell me the very first things that you see, or the very first impression that you have as you begin to understand where you are and what is happening around you. Tell me, what do you see in this new space?

Client D: Light.

Aliya: Okay, very good. That is Source light. How does it feel when you look at it?

Client D: Feels warm and encompassing all of me.

Aliya: Okay.

Client D: *Hmm.* Holds all of me. It feels unconditional.

Aliya: Very good. We're just going to pause and just let you get your bearings and let you bask in the presence of the Divine. (A few moments later) Okay. Ask Source, if we can ask questions?

Client D: Can we ask questions? Can we ask the questions that we have? *Yes.*

Aliya: It's important to remember that any voice that you hear in your head is the voice that we're connecting with. And we remember this as true. Okay?

Client D: *Mmh hmm.*

Aliya: <Client D> has started nurturing a connection with a loved one who's in spirit. The person crossed over at a young age, and she's wondering how they feel about her here on Earth keeping their spirit alive by holding onto their memories, photos, ashes or when memorials are created in their honor. How do they feel?

Client D: *They love it.*

Aliya: Okay, I thought so. I just wanted <Client D> to hear that.

The day before our session, Client D had posted a question to the spiritual group that we both belong to. "So, I've started nurturing a connection with a loved one who's in spirit. The person crossed over at a young age and I was wondering how they feel about us here on Earth keeping them alive by holding onto their memories, photos, ashes, or when memorials are created in their honor. Do we need to let go of them through these things or is it okay if we nurture them in these ways?" I'd suggested that this would be a great question to ask during our regression so that she could hear the answer directly from Source.

Client D: They love it. I feel a smile. I feel like they are smiling.

Aliya: And why do they love it?

Client D: So, I feel a bunch of them.

Aliya: Okay.

Client D: And it's a sense of acknowledgement that feels, like, they feel acknowledged and we (are) acknowledging them in the spirit world or the realm where they are.

Aliya: Very good. Who is <Client D> connected to, or who does she connect with?

Client D: They feel older than me?

Aliya: Elders?

Client D: They do. They feel like elders.

Aliya: Okay.

Client D: They feel, they feel proud of me for being the one that is brave enough to hold space for them, even when it seems crazy when I say things like, they're not here, but they are everywhere. They like that.

Aliya: Oh, good! How can she nurture these connections better?

Client D: *Hmm.* By connecting with myself and devotion to my practices.

Aliya: Oh, okay! Who is she connecting with in her dreams, or who is coming forth in her dreams?

Client D: *Hmm. There's no one right now.*

Aliya: Where is she going in her dreams?

Client D: *Different places. She's a traveler.*

Aliya: Okay, she thought… She feels that she's a traveler. Is there one specific place that she likes to travel to more that she should know about?

Client D: *Not really one specific place, but she enjoys the experience of visiting and traveling to multiple places. She's like a fly on the wall. Looking in, looking in on these places.*

Aliya: How can she better connect to loving relationships here on Earth?

Client D: *It always starts with self. Hmm! It starts with herself, and forgiveness and compassion and all of those things are in her purpose and so, it won't be easy, but it will be fulfilling. Because it's a purpose.*

Aliya: Okay, that was her… That was one of her questions. What is her purpose?

Client D: *Hmm.*

Aliya: So, what can she do to help with her purpose? What steps should she be taking to align with her purpose?

Client D: *Following her heart and intuition. Follow her inspirations. Keep asking questions. Keep talking to people, asking people questions. Hmm.* It's not very clear. But there's a sense that it lies within serving people, serving humanity.

Aliya: How will she serve humanity in this life?

Client D: *By being the light.*

Aliya: Okay.

Client D: *Hmm.* I see white. *I see her in white. It's not very clear all the way, but as long as she focuses on her light and using her light to help others, she should be okay. More than okay.*

Aliya: Good, good. So, is that her life's path?

Client D: *Hmm. For now.*

Aliya: Okay.

Client D: *For now.*

Aliya: She wants to know what her future holds for her.

Client D: *Joy. Many, many heart experience, heart opening experiences. Healing in the depths of her bones.*

Aliya: Is there a soulmate—

Client D: <inaudible>

Aliya: Oh, go ahead, finish!

Client D: *Also leading a family into not, per se, the right direction, but just leading a family in ways that are not very clear right now, not just leading them towards the light.*

Aliya: Okay. Is there a soulmate in her future?

Client D: *He's already...*

Aliya: He's already...? Has she met him?

Client D: *She knows him. She has met him.*

Aliya: Okay, good. What about children?

Client D: *They have one already. He has one, and they will have their own together.*

Aliya: Okay.

Client D: *She... It makes her happy to have a soulmate and his daughter in her life.*

Aliya: Oh, good!

Client D: *It makes her happy. And she wants to be a mother as well. She wants to connect the three of us in a way that she wants to connect the three of them and that's why she feels a strong connection to a spirit that's her own child or a child that is to come from her own womb with a soulmate.*

Aliya: And so that spirit has been hanging around her. She's been feeling it.

Client D: *She's just felt a strong connection to being a mother.*

Aliya: Oh, good!

Client D: *And she has had dreams before where they've visited her and to let her know... Those dreams let her know that there's a connection.* Someone is calling me.

Aliya: Yeah.

Client D: *Someone is calling her to... They want to be... They want... They're choosing her as their mother.*

Aliya: Oh!

Client D: *Even though here... Even though she's very scared. She's scared.*

Aliya: Does she have any reason to be afraid?

Client D: I don't know. *No, she doesn't. She doesn't. She's a Divine child. Was always protected.*

Aliya: Good. She's asking about her financial stability. What does that look like in the future?

Client D: *One word, abundance.*

Aliya: Oh, good! She was wondering about abundance, and how can she increase her abundance.

Client D: *Through her passions.*

Aliya: Okay.

Client D: *Her passions, and what sets her heart on fire and people. She has a very unique gift of connecting with people and specifically older people, elderly people.*

Aliya: Okay.

Client D: *She has this way of making them feel seen and not forgotten and heard and that doesn't easily translate with the younger generation. But she does know how she can connect with the younger generation, as well. It's just, there are blocks. There are blocks of the external validation, or just seeking the external? What is the external world going to think? What are they gonna feel? Because her soul is so old and so rich in wisdom. And so, she carries this, this, thing over where she feels like she cannot necessarily fit in with the younger generation because of how old the spirit feels...*

Aliya: Oh, that makes sense.

Client D: *...and so, it's easier to connect with the elderly people who care to listen, who care about wisdom. And she wonders about how to connect with people that are younger than the elders. Because she'd love to help them, too, at some point, she'd love to. She'd love to serve them, too, but she doesn't know how, yet. Because she feels the weight of the suffering that the world's also going through right now, and everyone else as well.*

And so, she doesn't know how to get through. She doesn't know how to get through to them, because they are so guarded.

Whereas, the elderly people, they're not so guarded. And so, you feel safer with them. But it does... It does weigh on her that she's, that she cannot get through to the younger ones, and these younger ones are, funny enough, a little bit older than her even. And so that is a factor, too. Like, how do you connect with someone who's older than you when they are so set in their ways already? But they're also not, and elderly at the same time. And so, she sees and she acknowledges it, and sometimes it even pains her. But that's just how big her heart is for people. And her being part of them as a people. So, that's her spirit right there.

Aliya: Can you help her to remove and clear those blockages?

Client D: More of those... breathing deep, deep breaths, deep breathing. Leaning on others. Allowing others to hold me. Hold space for me. But those blocks can be removed. It will just take some time.

Aliya: Okay. Thank you. Are there any blockages that can be removed today?

Client D: *She has been removing blocks since last night.*

Aliya: Oh, good!

Client D: *And it might not be those blocks that we are or that you are asking to remove today. But she's been removing blocks since last night. She's been removing or working through big blocks. Inner child blocks, and it's been triggering because her soulmate is the trigger but is not the cause of the trigger. And so those are the things that she's been learning and healing and moving through right now. But it hasn't changed the fact that it's still a soulmate. She's happy to be doing... She's happy to be moving through these things with him.*

Aliya: Okay.

Client D: *Because she hasn't had anyone hold her or hold her inner child the way they are being held right now. And so, she's been removing blocks. She's been moving through blocks. And so, I don't think I feel, I feel like she doesn't have the capacity anymore today to do. To remove those blocks. She's been doing a lot of work.*

Aliya: Can you please tell her what her soul's name is?

Client D: *She likes to be not necessarily called, but she, like, she resonates with the butterfly. She resonates with a butterfly. The lightness, the lightness of the butterfly. The... The transformations that a butterfly goes through. The ability to fly from place to place. She sees it as a form of traveling. Her spirit is so light, like a butterfly.*

And it's not coincidental that a butterfly came to sit on her the other day while she was doing nothing. Just looking at the sky and that butterfly felt so at ease. Just sat itself on her long enough to capture it on camera, and she knows that, what that moment meant between her and a butterfly. She knows exactly what it means, because once...

What happened in that experience is... Once she tried to show others that experience, the butterfly left as if it was never meant for anyone else but her. And so, she doesn't have a... Her spirit doesn't have a name because it's so multi-faceted or multi-layered, but she sees herself as a butterfly. She feels like a butterfly. They <inaudible> it like a butterfly, too.

Aliya: Okay.

Client D: *And most people don't know that about the delicacy of her.*

Aliya: She feels she has connections with angels. Can you please explain that for her?

Client D: *Numbers. Angels are connected to numbers. That's why she sees so many angel numbers.*

Aliya: And what are her angels... The names of those angels? Or that angel that she's connected with?

Client D: *Gabriel. Raphael. <laughter> Raphael, and Gabriel are the names.*

Aliya: Can you let her know how many times she's reincarnated?

Client D: *No.* <laughter>

Aliya: Why not?

Client D: *She's fixated... Her mind's fixated on knowing too much about that aspect. She's even... Her mind is even focused on the three hundred that you mentioned. Yeah, she's too fixated on the three hundred that was discussed prior, and so she is not allowed to know at this time.*

During our initial talk, before the regression started, while discussing what she wanted to gain from the session. Her or I had brought up young vs. old souls. I'd told her that while I didn't know how many times I'd reincarnated, the number was somewhere in the four hundred thousand range, but Source had described someone with a reincarnation of three hundred as young.

Aliya: But you've told her that she is an old soul.

Client D: *She knows that. She can feel it, too. She can feel it, too.*

Aliya: Okay. Okay.

Client D: *Not too old. But she's an old soul.*

Aliya: She does want to know (something about) her reincarnated lives. What has she reincarnated as or if you can tell her what's her favorite reincarnation? Is it human? Is it an alien? Is it a life? Is it plant? What is her favorite reincarnation?

Client D: *To be in nature. To be a part of nature.*

Aliya: How does she do that? Is it through a plant, or is it through animals?

Client D: *It's both. She's connected to the plants, and she has a connection to animals and children, too.*

Aliya: Okay.

Client D: *I see green, representing the plants.*

Aliya: She likes to be in nature?

Client D: *She loves it. She really loves it. She feels safe, she feels free. She goes free in nature and with the animals. She knows that's why they gravitate towards her. They feel safe with her. They know her spirit. The spirit is as sensitive as they are with the animals and children. She connects with him, too, in a very childlike way. Because she likes... She loves to play. She loves to play.*

Aliya: Are there any secrets that you can give her that will help her on her journey?

Chapter Fourteen

Client D: *Hmm. Secrets, maybe not. But guidance. Ask, and you shall receive. She knows what that means. It happened to her the other day. She asked and she received. And this is what happens when a Divine child asks the Universe and trusts the Universe and puts everything that they know and believe into God, the Universe and Spirit.*

Aliya: Thank you for that. I have a question for myself. What synchronicities am I seeing that can confirm that I am on my right path, and that everything is going as planned?

Client D: *Things happening in twos. Even threes. Doubles, seeing doubles of things. Thinking, speaking, and it appears. The tongue, a manifester's tongue.*

Aliya: Manifester?

Client D: *Manifester's tongue.* And so, speak things into existence, is what I'm getting. *However, who is this advice or this guidance for? Is it for you, Aliya, or is it for <Client D>?*

Aliya: For Aliya.

Client D: *For Aliya: Things happening in twos. Twos, threes and a manifester's tongue. So, whatever you say holds weight, holds power... And... Can you ask your question one more time, please, Aliya?*

Aliya: What synchronicities am I seeing as a confirmation that I'm on the right path, and that things are fine?

Client D: *Encounters like this, with her. With <Client D>. People's stories aligning with what's in your heart. Synchronicities like the right people ending up on your doorstep and you only know that they are meant to end up on your doorstep by listening to them speak, listening to their story.* But manifester's tongue is what I'm getting, so watch your words.

Never take them for granted, because your words hold power, like all of ours, do. But at the sense that you can speak things into existence and we possibly, we probably all can. But this is for you.

Aliya: Okay.

Client D: *This is for you. Definitely.* And things happening in twos as well. Twos, threes. That's what I'm receiving for you.

Aliya: Okay. Thank you. Thank you.

Client D: *You're welcome. You're so, so welcome.*

Aliya: We are going to thank Source for all the wisdom and guidance and we're asking Source to please, before we leave, to fill us with hope, love and just rain abundance down on us. And remove fear and doubt, especially fear and doubt within ourselves, and our life and our path and just give us blessings. Always help us do the right thing as we're called to connect with people and to enlighten people, and just to let our light shine brighter, that those people find us.

Client D: *So shall it be.*

Aliya: Thank you. So, we are going to leave Source here. But I want you to remember that you can always come to visit Source when you are trying to meditate, all you have to do is just remember this healing light in your body and ask Source to calm your mind so you can meditate and receive your gifts, and the knowledge that you seek.

Client D: I will. I do.

Aliya: What we're going to do now is, we are going to move forward and at the count of three, you are going to be in the presence of your Spirit Guides. You're going to be wherever you want to be to meet your Spirit Guides. One. Two. Three. You are with your Spirit Guides. What do you see or feel?

Client D: I feel a throb in my chest and the strong familiar feel(ing of being) connected to my soulmate because the question I asked in the group is connected to my soulmate, too. And I feel like… So, the person I asked about in the group is my soulmate's brother. He has passed on, I think, a couple of years now. I know, he passed on when he was ten, he's twenty-one now, he would have been on Earth. And I've always...

I'm nurturing a connection with this spirit now. But I've always felt okay and safe to speak about him so much that my soulmate has become comfortable with allowing himself to process his brother's passing. *And so that's why she asked that question in that group last night, because she doesn't want to do something that is detrimental to herself, her soulmate, or his brother.*

Aliya: Is her Spirit Guide his brother?

Client D: His brother is here right now.

Aliya: Good. Okay.

Client D: He's a newly added Spirit Guide. He wasn't always there.

Aliya: Okay.

Client D: He wasn't always a Spirit Guide. Maybe... *That's because they didn't always know they were soulmates. They were friends. They were friends first and once they realized what this actually is, she realized who he is, actually.* And so that's why he's a new Spirit Guide with us.

Aliya: Okay.

Client D: *He is getting to know her, but so is she. She speaks to him a lot. She speaks to him as if he's here. Which he is.*

Aliya: He is, he is there.

Client D: Thank you, very much.

Aliya: So—

Client D: *He is, he is. She's—*

Aliya: Does it—

Client D: *Same, like—*

Aliya: No, go ahead. Finish. I'm sorry.

Client D: *She speaks to him like she can see him. And she loves looking at his face. She loves that, and she loves the possibility of bringing this light into their family because there's a lot of heaviness. And the reason why she asked that question in the group is because she initially feels like she needs to lighten the spirits around his passing.*

Aliya: Okay.

Client D: *They are. They feel it very heavily, in a very dark sense, and I think they're still moving through that darkness of death. Nobody realizes that he's actually in the light.*

Aliya: Okay.

Client D: *So, if she feels like she sees it. Actually, she perceives it this way actually. She can see it like a dark cloud, and it's not necessary to hold on to that dark cloud anymore because she knows where he is. His family just doesn't know anymore. Not anymore.... They just don't know that he wants to come through as a light, but they're holding on to this darkness. So, it's kind of hard for him to penetrate not having a source, and she is the source.*

Aliya: Okay.

Client D: *She is the source and she just found that out now, but she always had an inclination that this is, this is the light that is about to enter their family. I mean, they do have light in their family.* That's my soulmate's daughter. She is the light in their family. *But why he has become a new Spirit Guide, and why he's getting to know her, and why she feels...*

Aliya: <Client D>.

Client D: Right?

Aliya: We lost you for just a minute, but you're back now, so everything is fine.

Client D: Okay.

Aliya: Does he have any advice for you?

Client D: He knows what his brother is like, and he knows that I know.

Aliya: Okay.

Client D: And not to give up on him and I see why. *She knows why and he doesn't...* He wants me to continue to encourage his brother to process it. Speak about it, talk about it, cry about it. Essentially, because the Spirit Guide, <name redacted>. His name is, <name redacted>. <name redacted> wants to see his brother on the other side of understanding death. <name redacted> wants his brother to know that death is only final to the human experience.

So, I think <name redacted> wants to connect with his brother and he's doing it through me and his (her soulmate's) daughter. I don't know why his daughter. I'm still getting to know his daughter, because we've only recently found out literally <the prior month> that we are soulmates, and so it's only unfolding now, and so I don't have... *She doesn't have a connection yet with his daughter enough to know that...enough to notice when <name redacted> is moving through his daughter, and she has the...*

She has the ability to notice that. She can see energy move like that Divine presence. She has that capability or ability. But because she is still getting to know this little girl, she's not as present and as active in order to see the Divine thread being worked through her. But what she is aware of is, she feels <name redacted> presence, and she feels him trying to connect with his brother through her.

Aliya: Okay. Okay. Okay.

Client D: *And sometimes she worries that she's crazy, too, like she's imagining it all. But...*

Aliya: Sure, I too, grapple with, "Am I crazy?" And I have to tell myself that as well. I'm not crazy. It's just, we are opening and expanding our human brains, and our human brains can't process everything that's out there.

Client D: Truly, truly. I mean, how do you... How do you process a Divine presence?

Aliya: Exactly.

Client D: It's beyond all of us. It really is. It is.

Aliya: Yes. Does your Spirit Guide have anything that they want to tell you before you guys part ways?

Client D: He sees me.

Aliya: Good.

Client D: He sees me. And acknowledges me. He might not know me fully, but he sees me, and he acknowledges me, and I acknowledge him.

Aliya: Okay, do whatever feels comfortable right now with your Spirit Guide. Some people hug. Some people hold hands. Some people talk briefly and exchange information that will stay between you and your Spirit Guide. I will leave you space to do that now.

Client D: He's right here.

Aliya: Oh, good. Okay, thank your Spirit Guide for coming through and for connecting with you. Now, at the count of three, we are going to move on, and we are going to move to the Akashic Records and just continue our journey. But there are two rules that we must abide by before we can move to the Akashic Records. Rule one is that we cannot look at anyone else's records but your own, and two, we must understand that the knowledge we seek must be for the good of all, and cause harm to none. Do you agree?

Client D: I fully agree.

Aliya: Okay.

Client D: At the count of three, we are going to be standing in front of the Akashic Records Library. One. Two. Three. You are now in front of the Akashic Records Library. What do you see?

Client D: Wow. There's so much. Yeah. I feel, I feel it. I feel more than what I see.

Aliya: What do you feel?

Client D: I feel vastness, if that's a way to put it, is vast. It's just so… It's so big. It's so abundant. It's so… I don't think I'm meant to see what it entails, but I'm meant to see what it looks like here. It's gold.

Aliya: Okay.

Client D: It's warm here. It's light here. It is... There's truth here. And there are gatekeepers of these truths, as well. I feel them.

Aliya: Okay.

Client D: I feel those gatekeepers, and they see me. They're not opening up for me, though. I am not ready to know what the space entails. Because I am still in awe of the space's presence. Yes, it's so... Yeah, it's very vast. And it's like, I'm gonna need to spend a couple of days here.

Aliya: <laughter>

It always amuses me and brings me immense joy when clients experience the Akashic Records for the first time. It makes me so happy to be able to witness the awe and wonderment of someone experiencing such a sacred space for the first time. And as an empath, I'm lucky to not only bear witness to this, but to also feel *the same excitement the client is feeling.*

Client D: Just sitting in awe, meditating and allowing the truth to come to me and not go search for it in this place and space, because I feel you don't come to search for the truth here. You come to *be* with the truth here.

Aliya: Very good. That's a good way of putting it.

Client D: You come to be with it. You don't come to search for anything. You don't come to receive anything. You just come to *be* with it. *Be* one with it. *Be* still with it.

Aliya: Okay.

Client D: And I respect that because if it's protecting me, then I'm okay with that. I am just grateful to be in a space that is exactly what I visualized it to be.

Aliya: Good. Okay, we are going to find your book. Your book should be coming to you, or you should be going to your book. But find your book. Do you see where your book is?

Client D: I see it. I feel it.

Aliya: I want you to get your book, and I want you to find a table or a chair, a comfortable chair. And I want you to sit and have your book in front of you. Let me know when that's done.

Client D: We are settled. The book is still closed. My hand is on the book.

Aliya: Good. What does your book look like?

Client D: It's weighted. It has a bit of weight to it. It is... It has a texture, a texture. I'm not sure which type of texture, yet, but it's textured. It has my favorite book smell and words and pictures.

Aliya: Okay, what does it say on the front of your book?

Client D: Wow! I see words. But something... I'm not sure what it's saying, like, I can see that there are words, but it's not speaking to me.

Aliya: It's okay, you just... We just have to unlock those memories. So, that's what we're gonna do now. You know what the words are saying, because you recognize the language because it is your home language. And you have those memories of how to read that language and how to speak that language in your head. At the count of three, we're going to bring those languages forward so that you can see exactly what it says. One. Two. Three. You now understand that language and those words. What does the front of your book say?

Client D: The story of <Client D's name>.

Aliya: Okay, very good. We are going to open to the first page of that book. And you tell me, what do you see there? Are there words there or are there pictures?

Client D: It's a picture.

Aliya: What is the picture?

Client D: It's a picture that moves.

Aliya: Okay. It's a life.

Client D: Yes, it takes me into... It's like a portal. The picture feels like a portal, and so it wants to take me into that portal to show me what this life was like.

Aliya: Do you want to go? That would be your first life. So, if you want to go and visit that life, we can pop in there.

Client D: We can. We should.

Aliya: Okay. So go ahead and go to that first page and tell me what you see.

Client D: I cannot see myself.

Aliya: What's around you?

Client D: *Hmm*. South African history, or just history. A time in history where... Vehicles were... Horses were vehicles. Women...were seen as one thing and one thing only, to bare children and fill in the blank. And sadness.

Aliya: Okay.

Client D: A woman with a blocked throat chakra. Sadness. Although, I can see her. She cannot see herself, but she's looking around. She's looking around. And the scene, it seems familiar. Like <Client D> today has even seen it in a movie somewhere. And even, and even when she saw it in a movie, it resonated. It resonated when she watched it. There's nothing particular about this life that she's here to see. But just to look, just to look around, look around and notice that this is where you've been once before.

Aliya: Okay.

Client D: And that's all I need to carry on with like digging in, unpacking, that timeline is too heavy right now.

Aliya: Okay, we're not gonna do that. Can we—

Client D: No.

157

Aliya: What is she in this life? Can she look down at her body to know what she is?

Client D: She's a woman.

Aliya: Okay.

Client D: She does things like washes, clothes, and cooks and is seen, not heard. Children also are safe with her. And she may have endured abuse even, to some degree.

Aliya: Since this life is too heavy for her, we're going to back out and go back to the Akashic Records. Are you there now?

Client D: I am.

Aliya: Okay, good. We want to see a life where she either had wings or was a butterfly. Does she have a life like that? If you have a life like that, then you would be able just to open up the book and find it.

Seeing a life (if she had one) where she had wings was a request from the client. Which is interesting since Source explained her connection to butterflies.

Client D: *Hmm!* She was a butterfly.

Aliya: Okay.

Client D: She was a butterfly.

Aliya: Why don't we go into that life?

Chapter Fifteen

Client D: *Hmm.*

Aliya: Are you there now?

Client D: Almost. It was beautiful. It wasn't easy getting to be the butterfly, but once she became the butterfly, she was free. Free in nature, and she loved being a butterfly because she could visit her loved ones like that. And she loved the fact that she could do that as a butterfly, and it's something she loves about butterflies today. In this present life, she loves that sometimes there's this magical, whimsical feeling of seeing a butterfly, and wondering is that her Spirit Guide? Is that a loved one? She loved that because she knows what that feeling felt like to be able to visit your loved ones in the form of a butterfly.

Aliya: That is special.

Client D: She loved that.

Aliya: Okay.

Client D: She could watch it forever. But butterflies never stick around for too long.

Aliya: They don't.

Client D: They don't, they don't. So, she thoroughly enjoys a butterfly experience.

Aliya: Oh, good! Good! Let us back out of that life. Go back to the Akashic Records. <Client D> now wants to see a life… If she had a life where she abused free will or abused her power or where her Karma lies. Please open up the book and find that page.

Client D: She was a male.

Aliya: Okay.

Client D: She was a male, man, that knew their power and knew the weight of it and used that knowingly, that it was not full of good.

Aliya: Okay, what time period is this?

Client D: Could be… It doesn't feel too old, but it doesn't feel too new, either. So, it could… The timeline feels before her earthly birthday which is in this current life. So somewhere, before she was born into this current life. She was… She was a male in power.

Aliya: Is she seeing that life? Is she in that life right now?

At this point, the way the client is describing things, I'm wondering if she's truly immersed in that life, or if she is just an observer. Usually, when clients are experiencing a past life, they immediately see themselves or think of themselves as "that" person. So, the way they speak is in first person; "I see". "I am", etc. But since she is speaking in third person, I'm not sure. And what's also confusing is she'd stated the life we were currently viewing was a male, yet, the client is referring to the spirit in that life as feminine.

Client D: She's seeing it. Yeah, she feels it, too. She feels it, too.

Aliya: What do her hands look like in this life?

Noticing that she's not connecting to this life, meaning, she's not seeing this as her *life, I used some techniques that I learned to help ground the client to the life we're trying to view.*

Client D: Strong, big, big fisted. The spirit was very determined. And…like… And it probably explains why she is so compassionate today when it comes to people. No matter what they did. She still finds a way to understand them, understand what makes them tick, what makes them do the things they do. And it feels like, because of this experience, she did not care at all. She couldn't care in this experience. In this past life, she couldn't care. She did not care about compassion, people's feelings, people's emotional state. She hadn't... She had a high.... To this day, in this current moment, she has a high emotional intelligence. She had it in the spirit's life as well, but it was misused.

Aliya: Okay.

Client D: It was misused and so, she knew back then what she was working with and used it not for the greater good. Instead, it was...suffering was inflicted onto the greater good by her. And so, her karma looks like that, forgiveness, learning to forgive, learning the hard way to forgive, in today's time. Her karma looks like learning forgiveness, the hard way. Learning to have compassion, the hard way. Learning to... Learning to hold space for other people, the hard way. And that is her karma. Her karma lives within people and treating them right.

Aliya: Okay.

Client D: Because of this misuse of power and the beauty of her life right now, is that she has the free will to do it. Her reward in this life is free will, so she can either repeat with this free will... With this free will, she can either repeat her past and that's why that life feels so... It feels... It doesn't feel that old, like the first life or the second, but the third one feels very close, very close. And so that is why it's so...there's such a strong feeling...and so, in this current life, this in the present moment, she can either use her free will to repeat the past life or she can redirect it and use that free will to heal what was broken. What made her that way in our past?

Yeah, what caused it to be that way? And so that is what's unfolding for her now is realizing that people are not meant to be used. They are meant to be loved. We are meant to use things and love people and not the other way around, and that is what that past life was like. Love things, use people. And that's why that statement, quote or saying rings so true with her because she can feel it from a deep place that you don't use people. You love people. You love people and you use things. And that's why she gets so mad, too, when she sees the reverse happening.

She…it's a trigger for her…it's not a trigger. But she gets a certain way. She feels a certain way when she witnesses and observes the reverse happening, when people use people, and they love money. So yeah, that's a karma from this lost past life experience. It's a very big one.

Aliya: It is a big one, but she seems to be in the space where she's fine. She's doing the right thing. She will get through it.

Client D: She is, and she will.

Aliya: Good. Okay, we're gonna now back out of that life and get back to the Akashic Records. Because our time here is almost coming to an end. But we want to spend time in the life that most connects… Oh, I was going to ask to spend time in the life that most connects to this life, but I think we just saw it. Is that correct?

We were nearing the three-hour mark of the session.

Client D: Yes, ma'am.

Aliya: Okay. So why don't we visit a life where she was happy and joyous and just surprise her with a life that she can carry in her heart space that gave her joy. So, find in the book, that life.

Client D: *Hmm.*

Aliya: What do you see?

Client D: A child with two parents that knows joy. That knows love. That knows two imperfect parents, but still knows love and support from two parents, and not just one. And that makes her inner child happy. That's why there's so much joy there in that experience, in that life. Because that's why there was joy. Because in today's life, that's what she doesn't have. That's what she's cultivating for herself and her own offsprings and that includes her soulmate's daughter. Her soulmate's daughter is included in that.

Aliya: Okay.

Client D: But, there was a time where she was joyful and a life where she's loved. She was a child, she was a child who experienced that much joy and the joy... And the joy stemmed from just having the love of two parents. Two present parents.

Aliya: What scene? What scene are you looking at right now?

Client D: What does that mean? What... I'm not...

Aliya: The life that you're seeing. What is going on in that life right now?

Client D: Just a child being actively watched over and paid attention to by the two parents.

Aliya: Okay.

Client D: By their parents...by this child's parents. Yeah, the parents are happy to just watch a child. Just be with a child.

I'm still not convinced that the client is fully grounded in any specific past life because she's still speaking as a viewer, she hadn't described a page in the book and I hadn't asked her to go into a life, I'd only instructed her to find one. I used the grounding techniques of asking about the specific person in the life to help her recognize that life as hers and her as the person she's viewing. Really, grounding helps to acclimate the client to the life as they are somewhat confused when they first "drop" into the life.

Aliya: What does the child look like?

Client D: It's a boy.

My heart leapt in my chest because I knew this boy and it was very apparent to me now that this little boy was following my energy, no one else. At this moment, so many thoughts were running through my head. This spiritual world that I was exploring was in fact, a fact. It was very real. What I'd meditated about was very real. Somehow, a very powerful energy was connecting to me and through me, also connecting to my clients, trying to be helpful as I worked.

My mind was blown. While the intent of this session wasn't to seek clarification for the existence of this energy, I'd definitely received it here. Even while writing this passage, I still can't put into words how my heart feels knowing that my voice was heard across the spiritual realm, and I'm loved so much that my soul baby is crossing time and space to help me.

Aliya: A boy? What does the boy—

Client D: <inaudible>

Aliya: What kind of hair does the boy have?

Client D: Very sleek.

Aliya: Okay is the boy... What color is the boy? What nationality or race?

I'm trying to find out if Client D will describe Noatok the same as the other two clients had and provide me with confirmation that this is truly Noatok coming through, once again.

Client D: I'm seeing a three-year-old, four-year-old, in age. Man, a really, really, sweet boy, for sure. And he seems... His race is not clear. But he's not very light, pale or White in skin color.

Aliya: Okay.

Client D: If that makes sense, yeah. So, he could be from any descent, maybe just not a White descent, because that's not the energy I'm feeling. I'm feeling... I just feel a very sweet child. That is just...That's just happy.

Aliya: What I'm going to do is, I'm going to try to connect you deeper into this life, okay? And when we go into this life, I want you just to be this person. So, on the count of three, you are this person. One. Two. Three. You are settled into the body of this person. Where are you from?

Client D: Brazil.

Aliya: Okay.

Client D: It has a native Mexican type of feel. I'm not sure.

Aliya: Okay. That's fine.

Client D: Just it's a brown, skinned baby.

While I had an inclining before that this boy she's describing was Noatok, by now, I am fairly certain of his presence. There was a sense of knowing and a lightness to my heart and I was excited to have him be present for yet another client.

Aliya: Awesome. And what is your name?

This question was meant for the client to state her name in the particular life she was reviewing.

Client D: What is your name? I'm getting a naughty smile. Like, I'm not gonna tell you my name. This kid is playing with me, and he's literally telling me, "I'm not going to tell you my name." <laughter>

I'm laughing here because I'm so full of awareness and I'm so joyful to be experiencing this magic. As stated at the beginning of this session chapter, I had closed bookings for my services so that I could connect fully to myself. But, two weeks before this session, during a connection with Source, I'd told Source that I was tired, confused and basically losing faith in my spiritual journey. My path was hard and while I had a great support system within my family, I felt very alone as spiritual journeys often are.

Still battling with the illusion of control, I'd given Source an ultimatum.

Source could turn things around for me by showing me a miracle (At this time my spiritual gifts were opening up and this new spiritual world was unfolding fast for me and I often flip flopped between, "I'm on a great magical journey." to "I'm absolutely insane and should be committed to a mental institution to get help to come back to reality.") or I was going to shut everything about this journey out, forget about my spiritual calling and re-join the corporate work force. HA!

I'd given Source a deadline. Source confirmed he (As a side note, Source shows up to everyone uniquely. For me, the energy is distinctively male. For others it might be female.) would show me a miracle by that deadline. The deadline had come and gone, leaving me distraught. I had cried, yelled and cursed at Source. I was upset that Source wanted me to trust myself, my visions, my intuitions, what I'm hearing and to trust these all as true. So, if I'm trusting this all as true, then I should be trusting it all, not picking and choosing what can be trusted, right?

So, if Source said he would meet my deadline, I trusted that I would have a miracle by a certain day. I had asked for a tangible miracle. I didn't want to see another feather, angel number, dream, vision, etc. I'd requested a miracle rooted in reality that, not only I could experience, but that others could experience as well (so that I could verify this with someone else and not feel alone and crazy. That day had come and gone without a miracle.

After my meltdown with Source, Source responded, "Forgive me, time doesn't flow the same. You'll have your miracle." The next day, I had my session with Client D. I was not expecting a miracle here. I was still waiting for my miracle (honestly, I was waiting for some kind of financial windfall to fall from the sky).

Aliya: Okay, so…

Client D: It's like he's playing a game with me. Like, *you know it.*

Aliya: Yeah, see, I think I know who this child is. Ask the child if it's Noatok.

Client: It is…should I? I'm sorry. What did you say earlier? Is the child Noatok?

Aliya: Noatok, is his name Noatok?

I truly understand that you, the reader, may think that by saying his name first, I'd led or swayed the client. However, the client didn't know about Noatok or his defining characteristics. I was certain this was Noatok for a number of reasons.

- *All clients describe him initially as, "a little boy".*
- *His age*
- *His nationality: Amazonian, Brazilian*
- *Trickster and playful energy*

Client D: Noatok? Yes. Yes.

Aliya: Okay, tell Noatok, I said, "Hi", and ask Noatok why he has come to visit us today.

Client D: She says, hi, Noatok! Why are you here today? He wants to hug me.

Aliya: Okay. Let him hug you.

Client D: Thank you. He wants to hug me.

Aliya: So, he does not talk. But you will feel his energy telepathically. Telepathically, he will speak with you.

Client D: Yeah. He wants to hug me. He went to… He's just so excited. Excited to have me there. Have his parents there. He wants to show me his parents. He wants to show me his toys. He wants to show me everything all at once and I don't know what I am to him. But he's just such a…

Aliya: What is he to you? What do you feel like he is to you?

Everyone he's connected with has a feeling of a very close connection to him. I'm curious who she thinks he is to her.

Client D: A sibling.
Aliya: Okay, he's your sibling.
Client D: A sibling.
Aliya: Ask Noatok. What is he to me?

Chapter Sixteen

Client D: What are you to Aliya? *Her son.* <laughter>

Aliya: <laughter> Yes.

Client D: Her son? What?

Aliya: My son. Yes, he is my son.

I am completely overwhelmed with emotion at this point in the session. During my meditation looking for answers, I'd connected with him, and he shared our story with me. But as mentioned in the previous chapter, I was going through a dark time of doubt and fear. So, although I'd connected with him and learned about our connection, I still had a trust problem and wavered between trusting and doubting my spiritual journey.

Having Noatok present with Client D wasn't surprising since he had already connected through three other clients before, but hearing him tell the client that he was my son—that was new. It left me feeling deeply validated. The private conversations I'd had with my spirit team in the spirit realm were now being confirmed openly by someone else. It made me feel... not so crazy anymore.

Aliya: Tell him, I love him very, very much. I'm so confused, though, about him. But I'm learning.

Client D: Oh! He loves you too!

Aliya: I love him, too. He only shows up when he wants to show you something, so take his hand and ask him what he wants to show you.

The fourth time is a charm! I'm getting the hang of what happens when he shows up. Any life the client had previously wanted to view? Forget it. Noatok was going to take the client's hand and lead them on an adventure.

Client D: I'm getting a warm bodily sensation right now.

Aliya: He's probably going to take you somewhere, so do you have his hand?

Client D: I do. I do.

Aliya: Okay, let him know that you're ready.

Client D: I'm ready. Noatok, let's go. Show me.

Aliya: He's going to take you to whatever you need to see, and you let me know when you get there.

Client D: I'm hearing, *sunset.*

Aliya: Okay.

Client D: A sunset.

Aliya: Okay.

Client D: And he just wants to sit on a bench with me. I'm seeing… I'm seeing a sunset horizon, a bench, and just me sitting with this little boy. His feet are just hanging, just hanging, and he's so… He's playful, but he's so content in silence and in quiet… He doesn't…

Aliya: Interesting.

Again, I'm coming into an awareness. I saw a bench in my vision. Not just any bench, but my *bench. My spiritual safe place, a place of peace and calm where I can connect to myself and rest. I'd been familiar with this deeply spiritual place for approximately thirty years.*

Client D: There with me. He's just sitting there with me. I feel safe with him. You feel safe. If we wanna talk, we will, we do that. But he's just happy with his feet dangling there. I think he actually just wanted to show me the sunset.

Aliya: Oh, okay.

Client D: He wanted me to see the sunset. Yes, he loves sunsets. I don't know why he enjoys sunsets. It's the end of his day, his play day right now.

A sunset can hold deep spiritual symbolism, often representing transitions, endings, and the beauty of impermanence. It's a moment when the day releases its energy, signaling rest, reflection, and surrender to the natural cycles of life. When Noatok showed Client D the sunset, it may have been a message of encouragement to honor a chapter that was coming to a close in my life (or hers) or encouraging me to find peace in the transitions I was experiencing.

The vivid colors and serene energy of a sunset can also symbolize hope, balance, and the promise of renewal, as night prepares the way for a new dawn. Sitting with Noatok during this moment suggests that he was there to provide support through this phase, reminding me that beauty and meaning can be found even in times of change.

And he's happy that we are at this bench. But still, his parents are waiting for him, waiting for him to finish up what he's doing. He loves that his parents are about him. He loves that they're present, they're active and there's this…one feels like feeling, feeling, yearning, and seeing. Not many words are being spoken in this lifetime, but there's a lot of feeling. There's telepathy, there's learning and there's seeing with this little boy.

And oh, man, he's just so sweet! Honestly. He has brown eyes…he does not have color, eyes. Oh, man, he's just a delicious chunk, that's all. He is a chunk of goodness.

Reader, take note of what Client D said in the section above, as we will revisit it in the Past Life Regressionist #2 session.

Aliya: Does Noatok have anything that he wants me to know or any messages for me?

Client D: He wants you to… He wants you to… But he knows that you're working through some things, and you're moving through some things, and he sees you. He sees you. He knows you. He knows that you know. And, you can play with him, too. Yeah, you can invite him into your play, whatever that play looks like for you. Because he loves to play.

Aliya: Yes, he does. He loves to play.

Client D: He loves to play, and I feel a sense of sadness. And when… It's the type of sadness where a son can feel his mother's sadness too.

Aliya: Oh!

Client D: *Hmm.* Yeah. He sees that, too. He feels that, too. And when you are going through those moments, he is there. He is there and he wishes he can touch you. He wishes he can touch you. He wishes he can just… You've probably felt his presence, but he wants to lay a hand on you, but that's why he just stays. He just stays. Yeah.

At this point, I had put my mic on mute because I was experiencing an emotional outpour that completely overwhelmed me. I was crying, feeling grateful for this connection with Noatok and with Source and grateful for being seen, heard and most importantly, loved. I was overwhelmed with love and confirmation that Source had heard me, and this experience that I currently lived through was, in fact, real and rooted in the here and now.

Aliya: Tell him, thank you.

It took effort to pull myself together and to continue the session.

Client D: She says, thank you. She says, thank you. And I feel her. Thank you, too. It's very deep. It's very raw. It's…it took a lot to say, thank you. It took a lot to say, thank you. No, it didn't take a lot to say, thank you. You held a lot back in order to say, thank you, in order to say, yes. There was a lot that you were holding back in order to say, thank you, without making it about you.

Aliya: Yes.

Client D: I feel that… I feel like the vessel between the two of you right now.

Aliya: You are. <laughter> I was asking for a miracle to come through and I was upset that I never got my miracle. And now, I'm wondering if this is my miracle?

Client D: It is, it is.

Aliya: I accept it.

Client D: Oh, happiness, happiness, happiness! The miracle was never going to look and feel the way you visualized it. But it came through in the best way possible that's going to fulfill you in ways…that won't feel like it right now. But with the goosebumps I'm feeling on my legs, I trust that with time, your acceptance will come with time.

Although I understood what was happening at this time, it would still take months for me to settle into the gravity of this moment.

Aliya: I agree.

Client D: And he's going to visit you more often after that.

Aliya: I wish he would visit me as often as he can, because I feel—

Client D: That's your invite. That is your invite, my friend. Go, visit her.

Aliya: Please. I've been calling him, but I'm not sure if he's been seeing me.

Client D: He wants to play with you.

Aliya: I would love to play with him. I need more play in my life. We all need more play in our lives.

Client D: Exactly, and that's why it's been hard for him to respond to your call.

Aliya: Okay.

Client D: That's why he wants to respond through play.

Aliya: Okay, I will play more then, because I've been noticing that I've not been playing as much as I should.

Client D: And we all do that, but just the awareness of it is everything.

Aliya: Yeah.

Client D: And now you have awareness and motivation.

Aliya: Yes, I do.

Play is an important part of any spiritual journey, spiritual awakening or being. If you're too uptight and can't see the beauty in playing and being open, there will not *be a spiritual journey, awakening or being. Everyone can choose to play as they see fit. Choose to do what makes you happy and do what brings you joy. For me, I play with tarot cards, with my phone, through creative expressions (writing, painting and crafting), exploring the spirit realm, having experiences with my friends and family and connecting with clients through psychic readings and past life regressions. I've since invited Noatok into those areas of my life.*

Client D: I love that. Wow! I love that I can be this for you right now, Aliya.

Aliya: Oh, thank you!

Client D: I've never done this before with anyone to this extent and to this depth. I've channeled before, but not in this way before. Like, solidly, I love this experience right now.

Aliya: I love this for you.

Client D: Oh!

Aliya: Okay. I don't want to make this about me. We're supposed to be looking at your life. What we're going to do, tell Noatok, thank you for showing up today and providing my miracle and renewing my faith in what I'm doing, and what I'm meant to do.

Client D: He heard all of that, and he receives all of it. You're so, so welcome.

Aliya: Okay, so we're going to leave him there, and tell him, I know what bench he's sitting at, and I would love to meet him there. That's my bench, so…

Client D: Oh, that's your bench! I had no idea.

Aliya: That's my bench. That's where I go, and that's where I go to connect.

Client D: Oh, wow!

Aliya: Just to myself, my Higher Self, and to my Spirit Guides. I go to a bench.

Client D: I had no idea.

Aliya: He took you there, and I am very grateful for you and for him, for this opportunity.

My safe place spiritually, is a field of green grass, sprinkled with plants and flowers. There's a path made of black gravel that runs from one end to the other and directly off the pathway is a wood bench. This is where I go spiritually to contemplate, receive messages, be within my own energy and enjoy myself.

While the essence of this place exists in the waking world as "someplace I used to visit as a child", I was first introduced to this spiritual safe place when I was in my early twenties.

During a dream (my dreams are either; regular fun dreams, a premonition or a lesson of some sort (which could also include meetings with my spirit team)), I'd been sitting on my bench, waiting for someone (who, I hadn't known at the time). So, I sat, kind of kicking my legs underneath me and looking around. The day was nice and sunny and the weather was warm. There was nothing going on, but I knew I was waiting for someone, and they would be coming from the left of the path. To the right, the path led through an open field that was beautiful as far as I could see. But to the left, the path led through a dense forest and the way was filled with fog. I couldn't see where the destination led that way.

As I sat there, just wondering why I was called to be there, I saw two figures approaching through the fog from the left of the path. As the figures came closer into view, I recognized the first as my Uncle Todd who'd died years earlier (at that time, I wasn't aware that he was one of my Spirit Guides). The second person was my Uncle Donnie, who'd also passed away years prior.

For years, my Uncle Todd had come to me in my dreams. His only request had been for me to tell my grandmother (his mother) that he loved her deeply and to let her know that he was in a much better place. I'd been resisting this message for years. He'd first started coming to me when I was eighteen, I hadn't been in touch with my spirituality at that point, let alone comfortable or even aware of all of my spiritual gifts. I was young and scared and certainly didn't want anyone thinking I was crazy for what I had to say or have such an emotional baggage levied on my grieving grandmother.

My grandmother, even years later, was still raw with her son's passing. My uncle had passed as a young man and his life had been a painful one. He'd had a lifelong chronic illness that left him in the hospital for most of his life. So much so, that he hadn't been able to attend regular school growing up.

At first, my uncle had asked me to relay messages to my grandmother, but years later, the asking became begging. Even now, I can still remember my uncle pleading with me. I just couldn't bring myself to put myself out there like that. Even after he stopped asking me to relay messages, he still came to me. In the dreams, it would be my uncle, my grandmother and myself, sitting in her living room, no one talked. We were only there enjoying each other's energy.

I want to note that during these dreams, my grandmother would be sitting on the couch, doing a crossword puzzle while my uncle and I were silent. I always knew that I was the connection, and my uncle just wanted to be by her, enjoying her space. I allowed this. It was also better for me since my uncle had stopped asking me to relay messages.

Now, back to me sitting on the bench and watching my uncles coming toward me. I was so excited to see them. My Uncle Donnie had never come to me before, so I was a little apprehensive to see him, but since he was with my Uncle Todd, I trusted he was who he presented to be (sometimes spirits aren't always who they present to be, but that's for another book). One thing to note about my Uncle Donnie's energy, was that he hadn't seemed as confident with being in such a space as my Uncle Todd had. It also felt as though the only reason he was coming through was to support his brother. My Uncle Donnie did not speak at all during this encounter and also did not really engage with me. He was just, there.

My Uncle Todd came closer, and we hugged. I was so happy to see him that I cried. While we both sat down on the bench, my Uncle Donnie stood off to the side. My Uncle Todd held my hand and told me over and over again that he was sorry. Sorry for asking me to relay messages to my grandmother, sorry for persisting and sorry for putting all that on me. I also apologized for not having the strength to tell my grandmother his messages. He told me that he should not have persisted for as *long as he had. He said that this would be our last time seeing each other in this way. I was very sad, and he said that he was just sorry and that he loved me and now that I'm thinking of it, I know he said other things, but I can't remember what. Maybe one day I will remember.*

Since then, I've learned that he is one of my Spirit Guides, and our connection is strong and beautiful. He still comes to me, but it's different now. It's in more of a Guide perspective, not an uncle. I'm forever grateful for my Guide and for him providing closure to that time period.

Ever since then, I've traveled to this space energetically. This space is my sanctuary. Sometimes I'm there, sitting on the bench by myself and sometimes I'm lying on my back, relaxing in the field and watching the sky. Neither of my uncles have ever joined me there again.

Client D: I can only appreciate this in silence right now. It's amazing. Wow.

Aliya: Yes. Okay, we're going to take a couple of deep breaths, because that was heavy.

Client D: It was.

Aliya: And then we're going to give both of us some of that Source healing.

Client D: *Hmm.*

Aliya: Just to help us be able to process the happiness, not relieve it, because we need it.

Client D: Process it.

Aliya: And transmute it and turn it into joy and happiness and confidence as we move on in our journeys.

Client D: *Hmm.*

Aliya: Okay. We're going to leave Noatok, tell him, thank you. And we are going back to the Akashic Records. One. Two. Three. You are back there now. Okay, we're going to put your book up where it belongs and we're going to thank The Keepers for allowing you to be in this space and to enjoy this space. And if you want to, or you need to, or if you want to look more into your life and your life's purpose, or to just visit and sit in the truth, that is the Akashic Records.

I want you to ask The Keepers if, since now that you know the rules and you were respectful of this place, if you could return, and then, when you want to return, if they can make that easy and possible for you. The Keepers do not have to be around you when you ask that question. They may come forward. If they do, they do, but if not, that's fine. That's just something you can ask in this space, your energy there, so go ahead and ask.

Client D: May I please return here in the right mind, in the right heart-space and if I do not show up for those energies then I accept that I have no business being you. But if I am, and you guys feel I am in the right space to be and please let it unfold, and let it be gracious. Let it be beautiful. Let it be fulfilling and please allow me to receive what there is to be offered up to me in knowing knowledge or wisdom.

I do not want to know what I am not allowed to know, and I am open to everything that I am meant to know. I am most grateful for this place and space. And if it's not too much to ask, I would love to be welcomed back here. I would love to be led back here through meditation or any other modality or practice. I would love to be led here, and if not, that's also okay. This was enough for me. And wanting more. That would be outside of my enough. And so, I'd love to be back here. But I am most grateful for this experience. So shall it be.

Aliya: *Hmm.*

Client D: *Hmm.*

Aliya: Okay, have they answered you?

Client D: *Time.*

Aliya: Time? Okay.

Client D: *Digest this right now. Work. Work on your practices.* And I'm not... I'm not being denied. I'm not being denied. I just need to come through the proper channels next time, and this is definitely one of them. Don't get me wrong. This is the perfect channel. And I would do this again. But doing it or accessing this place and space on my own.

Aliya: Yes.

Client D: That... That's what they mean by access it through the right channels. Don't try to bypass anything. Don't come in the wrong mind frame, heart frame. That...that's what my access granted means. And so, I'm not...I'm not denied. But these are the things that they want me to come forth or embody before I come here or visit this place again. And I accept that. I accept.

Aliya: Okay, and I would like to tell my friend, who is a Keeper, hello.

My relationship with The Keeper is noted in the passages below.

Client D: Oh, thank you, thank you for her. Thank you for you and thank you for welcoming me into this place and space moment.

Aliya: Okay, at the count of three we're going to exit because our time here is coming to an end. One. Two. Three.

I left this session feeling better than I had in a long time. I'd received confirmation about who Noatok was and who he was to me and also my faith in Source was restored. I could trust Source, Noatok and myself. Although the miracle hadn't come in as I'd imagined, I was satisfied to have received tangible evidence that someone other than myself could verify what was happening to me spiritually. I had a soul baby connected to me. Now, it was time to find out more about him and what my job was (if any) to help foster our connection.

Chapter Seventeen
Aliya
Past Life Regression: 05-NOV-2024

One of the groups I belong to is of trained past life regressionists. This is a group where we discuss what we've encountered, answer and ask questions and practice past life regressions on each other. I'd reached out and asked to be regressed into lives with Noatok. It was time to stop being lazy about my connection and investigate what I saw, heard and experienced.

The next transcripts are from two past life regression sessions that were done on me from other past life regressionists. I've removed all instances where the regressionists asked their own personal questions for Source as those questions are irrelevant for this book. Contact info for them both can be found at the end of this book.

I'd provided to the regressionist, the life that I'd wanted to see, my list of questions for Source and a list of spiritual gifts that I'd wanted Source to unlock for me.

Past Life Regressionist #1: Let's try to move one step closer to moving into your life with Noatok. I'm going to help you move your soul into the life that you want to see with Noatok. On the count of three, you are going to feel yourself moving quickly into the life you want to see with Noatok. It may feel like an energetic pull as you move to where you need to be and once I get to three, you will feel your feet hit the ground in the space you need to go with Noatok. One. Two. Three. You have now moved into a life that you have lived with Noatok. Tell me, what do you see or feel around you?

Aliya: I'm somewhere, but for the life of me I cannot see.

Past Life Regressionist #1: Do you feel something?

Aliya: I feel a little nervous and anxious. Not a whole lot, but that's what I feel.

Past Life Regressionist #1: Okay.

Aliya: I'm not anywhere, but when you're talking, like, I felt that I left wherever I was, but I'm like, in this…kind of looks like the aurora borealis. Yeah, like, I'm there… But I don't know where "there" is.

Past Life Regressionist #1: So, do you feel anybody around you? You feel like, maybe Noatok is beside you or anywhere near?

Aliya: No, I don't feel anything.

Past Life Regressionist #1: Okay.

Aliya: I've never had this feeling before, so I don't know.

Past Life Regressionist #1: Yeah, that's okay. We'll figure this out. So, what lights do you see in that aurora borealis?

Aliya: They're just fading in and out, nothing… Oh, well, now, I'm getting all this red… Hold on, I'm getting like, fire.

Past Life Regressionist #1: Okay. Is this an actual fire?

Aliya: No, it's just like flashes of… I have it somewhere else.

Past Life Regressionist #1: Can you describe to me where you are?

Aliya: I don't think I'm in an actual place. And that's confusing me.

Past Life Regressionist #1: Do you think maybe you are just a soul in the spirit realm?

Aliya: Yeah, just and kind of a nothing.

Past Life Regressionist #1: So, in this nothing where you are. I want you to go find the energy, the essence, the soul of Noatok. And let's see if he can help us figure out where we are and what is happening.

Aliya: Okay.

Past Life Regressionist #1: Can you go and find this energy? Do you feel it anywhere? Can you feel his energy anywhere?

Aliya: I think he's telling me I'm not supposed to be here.

Past Life Regressionist #1: Why not? Can you ask him? Is he saying something?

Aliya: Yeah, he's saying, *"It's because there's nothing here."*

Past Life Regressionist #1: Can you ask him if there is a life that you have lived together?

Aliya: He says, *"You live your life, and I live mine."* Mmmm... Let's see...

Past Life Regressionist #1: Okay.

Aliya: I'm asking if we have a life together. And he said, he doesn't live, lives.

Past Life Regressionist #1: Okay.

Aliya: I don't know what that means.

Past Life Regressionist #1: Does he mean that he doesn't live physical lives?

Aliya: *Correct.*

I've since learned that we have at least one life that we shared, which is explored during the Past Life Regressionist #2 section.

Past Life Regressionist #1: So, can you express to him your desire to feel or embody time with him to...

Aliya: He says...he says, *"We connect all the time."* He's holding my hand. He says, *"We connect all the time. We stay in connection with each other."*

Past Life Regressionist #1: Can we ask him a couple of questions that you prepared?

Aliya: *Mmh hm.*

Past Life Regressionist #1: Okay, so can he explain his relationship to you?

Aliya: He just laughs. He's saying, I'm his mother. I just have to trust. What's weird to me is that since this, like, I'm nowhere... I'm like wondering if I'm having this conversation with myself, so I'm just trying to just go with it, because I don't know. It's so weird.

What's funny is in preparation for the past life regression sessions that I lead, I counsel clients that they will feel weird. They will think they're making everything up and to just trust the process and go with the flow, yet here I am, questioning the process as well. I'm well aware of the hypocrisy of it.

Past Life Regressionist #1: Yeah, I understand. But just, let's just trust what is happening right now.

Aliya: Okay.

Past Life Regressionist #1: And let's just, whatever comes to you, whatever you feel or hear, we're going with that. Okay, alright. Can you ask him why he has come into your life when he did?

Aliya: He said, *"Pain and difficulty."* And he's kind of cradling my head and stroking my hair and telling me, this is a hard time, and I called out for help. So, he's here to help me. He heard... He heard my call.

As I've mentioned a few times already, so far, my spiritual journey has been a scary and lonely one. There were three distinct instances where I was so energetically drained that I'd verbally called out into the ether for help. I did it once during prayer, once during mirror shadow work and once during a past life regression session speaking to Source. I can't say which of those was where Noatok heard my call, or maybe it could have been during all three times. As someone who'd previously moved through life as a fiercely independent individual, I didn't ask for help often. I used to think I could do everything myself if I dug deep enough to find the strength. But this spiritual journey thing? I found that I needed spiritual help and a lot of it. I was at my wits end and life had been particularly hard during this time.

Past Life Regressionist #1: How can he—

Aliya: He's...he's saying that the help... He's saying the help is different. He's giving me the help I need, not the help I want.

Past Life Regressionist #1: What does the help look like? The help you need?

Aliya: He's saying... *"Bigger...bigger picture."*

Past Life Regressionist #1: Can he expand on that?

Aliya: He's saying, he's putting things into place. I can't tell what he's putting into place but looks like he's arranging things. He's saying... Yeah, just things being put in place.

Past Life Regressionist #1: He is helping with that, is that correct?

Aliya: Yes.

Past Life Regressionist #1: Is there a way that you can help him? Or is there anything you should do to help him?

Aliya: He said, that his job would be easier if I would just trust myself more.

Past Life Regressionist #1: What job is he talking about?

Aliya: Yeah, he's just trying to put things in place, and then he's showing my hand, swiping it away.

Past Life Regressionist #1: Can he expand on what kind of things he's putting into place or give an example of something concrete that can help you trust the process more?

Aliya: He just...he just wants me to put my hand down, and just let it be.

Past Life Regressionist #1: Okay.

Aliya: So—

Past Life Regressionist #1: Go ahead.

Aliya: No, I think that was it.

Past Life Regressionist #1: Alright. Can you ask him what you should be doing now?

Aliya: He's saying there's nothing for me to do. It's all…it's already happening, there's nothing for me to do. He just says, he wishes I would be able to see everything. I guess I'm very close-minded and kind of in the box and I'm thinking I'm fighting to get out of the box, but I don't have to fight to get out of the box. Everything is all open. If I can just lift up my head and look and see that I'm not in a box, that like, it's so much more that I could see. But my very limited thinking has me focused on this small world of Earth.

Past Life Regressionist #1: Is there anything he can do to help you now to open your mind more to everything outside of that box, to help you lift your head and see?

Aliya: No. He's saying, they show me everything. I'm not in a box. I'm actually…my head is up in the clouds, I'm there. It's just, I keep thinking I'm in a box, but I'm not anymore.

Past Life Regressionist #1: So, you're limiting yourself.

Aliya: I'm very scared about… He said, "*Humans.*" I'm very scared about human stuff. I'm like, he's showing me crouched down. Just head down, crouched down. So, sometimes my head's down and sometimes my…I'm up, and I'm above the clouds. So, he's just showing me both versions of myself, and I think this…I'm swinging on both, but…

Past Life Regressionist #1: Is there anything he can…any advice he can give you for that? Can he help you to trust the process in this life more and trusting yourself more?

Aliya: I just like…he's just patting me up. But he's not worried about me. I guess, eventually, I'll just know. I don't know why I'm fighting this so hard. But… Yeah.

Past Life Regressionist #1: Do you feel like you're trying to block the message that's coming through?

Aliya: No. It's just, I guess, making sure things are supposed to go off as planned. I guess it's just, you know, me being stubborn and kind of like, knocking big buildings... and then knock it over because I want things a certain way.

Past Life Regressionist #1: Okay. Alright.

Aliya: He's just saying, there's more to it than what I can see. So, I'm, I guess, I'm knocking things over because I wanted to come in as human and see it as human as possible. But they build stuff, and then I don't recognize it or something, and I knock it over.

Past Life Regressionist #1: Okay. Alright. Well, thank you. Thank him for explaining that to us. Is there any way that he can show you or give you the experience that you've wanted to see of you spending time with him?

Aliya: I'll ask him... I just asked him what life with him is like, and now everything is very white and bright and just, my heart is filled with love.

Past Life Regressionist #1: Beautiful. So, is that the feeling that you have when you spend time together in your life?

Aliya: Yes

Past Life Regressionist #1: Beautiful. Is there anything you do here together, or is it just being?

Aliya: Just being.

Past Life Regressionist #1: Wonderful. Okay. Well, thank him for his time and his answers and him helping you figure some things out and answering your questions. I actually have another question for him, if that's possible. If he's still there. Why has he been showing up in your regressions with other people?

Aliya: Because I'm open. That's the time where I'm open, and if someone else experiences it, then it's... I'm more able to trust that it's him, and it's true. If someone else says it and not me, then I get on board with it.

Past Life Regressionist #1: Okay, that makes sense. Is there anything else he wants to say before we move on to Source?

Aliya: Just, that he loves me.

Past Life Regressionist #1: Beautiful.

Aliya: And that he's proud of me for doing this. He knows it wasn't easy.

Past Life Regressionist #1: That's beautiful. Well, thank Noatok for his time and his energy and we will now say goodbye to him. I'm sure he will see you soon again, but we will now, in this moment, move on and move forward to go to Source. So, we are leaving this space with Noatok behind, and we are moving forward to go to Source. On the count of three, you are going to find yourself in the direct presence of Source. One. Two. Three. You are now present with Source. So, tell me, do you feel the energy of Source present in this new space?

Aliya: Yes.

Past Life Regressionist #1: What does Source look like to you?

Aliya: It's red everywhere. I just…a bright red light. There's something else there, but I can't make it out. It just keeps like popping in and out of my vision.

What I'm not relaying to the regressionist is that I'm trying to force my brain to see Source how my clients tell me that they see Source; as a bright white light. What I also haven't relayed to the regressionist is that I have a history and problem with trying to control everything. It's something I struggle with in my 3D life as well as in my spiritual life. I'm working on trusting the process and going with the flow, but obviously, I still have more releasing of control to do. So, the difficulty in meeting Source was entirely on me and not the regressionist.

Past Life Regressionist #1: Can we focus on what's popping in and out of your vision? Let's pinpoint that energy and let's figure out what that is. If you focus more on the energy, can you see more clearly what is popping in and out?

Aliya: Not at this time.

Past Life Regressionist #1: Okay.

Aliya: It turned white then it turned red again.

Past Life Regressionist #1: The energy around you?

Aliya: Yes. It's bright, bright, bright, bright, bright, bright, bright. I think it's popping in or don't know, if that was letters, but I can't really tell, or numbers? I can't tell what that is.

Past Life Regressionist #1: So, let's focus instead on the feeling of Source around you. What does Source feel like for you?

Aliya: It's changing like it goes from red to bright white.

Past Life Regressionist #1: Let's move into that bright white light. Let's stay there and feel into that energy and that presence. Can you feel yourself in the white light?

Aliya: Yes.

Past Life Regressionist #1: Does this feel like Source for you?

Aliya: Yes.

Past Life Regressionist #1: What does it feel like?

Aliya: It's familiar.

Past Life Regressionist #1: Do you still see things popping in and out?

Aliya: It'll go away, and then it will come back. Right now, it's not there.

Past Life Regressionist #1: Do you feel like the energy you are in is one being or one energy?

Aliya: I don't…. I don't know if… like… I gotta go back. I don't know if I'm there anymore.

Past Life Regressionist #1: Do you feel like the red color was more the energy of Source?

Aliya: Yeah.

Past Life Regressionist #1: Okay, so let's go back to the red color. We're moving back into the red color to meet the energy of Source. Do you feel yourself in that red color?

Aliya: Okay, I'm back at Source.

Past Life Regressionist #1: Can you repeat that, please?

Aliya: I'm back at Source.

Past Life Regressionist #1: Okay, great. Is it possible to ask Source a couple of questions?

Aliya: So, I'm getting frustrated because it was there and now, I'm back in blackness. So, I'm gonna see if I can call Source again.

Past Life Regressionist #1: Okay. Yes. Let's call Source again. Let's move back and ask Source to join you, so you can find yourself in his presence again. Can you let me know if you feel any different? Is there anything changing for you? Any energies you are feeling?

Aliya: It's just being in and out. I can't… For some reason, I don't know. I can't hold on to Source. Don't know… I don't know why.

Past Life Regressionist #1: Let's ask Source to make his presence known to you more deeply and more intuitively. So, you can access his wisdom more clearly and more easily. Let's ask your spirit team to help you move into Source without trouble and without any worries or interference. Tell me, are you feeling any different?

Aliya: Yeah, I think I'm in front of Source.

Past Life Regressionist #1: What does it look like for you?

Aliya: Just white light.

Past Life Regressionist #1: Can you ask or see if we can ask Source your questions?

Aliya: Yes.

Past Life Regressionist #1: What is Aliya missing as far as making her psychic practice grow and start to pick up with paying clients?

Aliya: *Nothing. Just let it be. It will, it will grow where it's supposed to grow.*

Past Life Regressionist #1: Do you have a timeline for this?

Aliya: *So stuck on time. But it's not her time. It's Divine timing.*

Past Life Regressionist #1: What alien did she see in her bedroom back in 1991? And what was the purpose of that encounter?

Aliya: It was just curious. It follows my family— It's from a different realm.

Past Life Regressionist #1: Why?

Aliya: Because we're easy. Our family is easy to track, because of our light.

Past Life Regressionist #1: And what alien is it? What species?

Aliya Griffin

Chapter Eighteen

Aliya: I can't say the name. I don't know what the name is, and Source is telling me that it doesn't matter. I wouldn't (know how to pronounce it or recognize it)…anyway.

Past Life Regressionist #1: That's okay. So, can we take some of the unnecessary pain, anxiety, fear, remorse, sadness, and stress? Can we take that away and replace it with confidence, peace, self-love, happiness, and joy for Aliya?

Aliya: Source is saying <laughing>, that I want to take everything away that makes me human.

Past Life Regressionist #1: Is there anything?

Aliya: No, it's just that… I think I don't need these things, but I actually do need these things because they make me, part of me.

Past Life Regressionist #1: Yeah. It's part of the human experience. Is that correct?

Aliya: *Yes.*

Past Life Regressionist #1: Is there anything we can do at this moment with the help of Source to ease some of those pains and anxieties and sadnesses to help it be less intense for you?

Aliya: Source is saying that, I know I don't want to hear it but, things aren't as intense as I think they are…is…I'm doing this to myself. It's showing me the box again that I'm putting myself into. But it's a box with no walls, like I'm miming it (the walls). But there's nothing there. There's nothing holding me back. I'm free. I'm just not moving into this space.

Every time I have a perceived problem that I realize isn't really as big of a deal as I've made it out to be, I think of the vision Source showed me, miming the walls of a box and I crack myself up.

Past Life Regressionist #1: Is there any advice Source has that can help you move yourself out of that imagined box?

Aliya: Source said, *"In time."* They aren't...

Past Life Regressionist #1: Okay.

Aliya: They aren't concerned about me, like they... I'm here and they're just showing me like, yawn and stretch, like, in time, I'll figure it out. It's part of the process.

Past Life Regressionist #1: Can you ask Source, what your gifts are, and which ones can be strengthened today?

Aliya: Source said, I already know my gifts, and I asked to strengthen them. So, they're strengthening them right now.

During previous regressions, I'd confirmed my gifts are: clairvoyance, clairaudience, claircognizance, clairsentience, empath, telepathy, medium, precognition and channel.

Past Life Regressionist #1: How long will that take?

Aliya: We don't have to wait. Source is just saying, I have all the necessary tools, but I just keep wanting more tools, and I keep wanting to just hop to the next thing without like... I'm collecting tools like, I'm collecting all this stuff, and I don't really know how to use them all so it's making me quite confused.

Past Life Regressionist #1: Okay. Alright.

Aliya: I'm being impatient.

Past Life Regressionist #1: Can Source, help you with patience?

Aliya: Learning it. I'm doing it myself. I have to do everything myself. I'm learning it, and I'm doing it good. It's just... I'm being impatient with me.

Past Life Regressionist #1: Okay.

Aliya: So, it's a *me* thing.

Past Life Regressionist #1: Alright. Okay. So, can we unlock gifts such as telekinesis, remote viewing, astral projection, seeing aura or seeing portals?

These were the spiritual gifts I'd provided to the regressionist, wanting her to get Source to activate them for me. Source saw through me from the beginning and called me out about collecting spiritual gifts and confusing the heck out of myself.

Aliya: *She doesn't need telekinesis. She astral projects all the time.*

Source is correct, I do astral project often. But I'd wanted to astral project more. *I have all these spiritual gifts and sometimes I get in my head that I want more of them. More clear sight. More knowing. Just...more.*

She already knows how to remote view, she just has to relearn it. See... Everyone can see portals. They're all around us. The issue is that we are looking with human eyes. So, we... Our brain fills in the space to what makes sense to the brain.

What's not communicated to the regressionist is that I was having a sidebar with Source. Source asked, "What would you do with telekinesis anyway?" And my answer was, "Mind your business." So, no, I didn't get that spiritual gift. That apparently was the wrong answer.

It's also important to note that everyone should cultivate their own personal relationship with Source. My relationship with Source is one of love, understanding, playfulness and security. Our relationship sometimes is one of a wise old man and the brat or teacher and student. I talk to Source multiple times a day and Source answers. I think it's important to divulge this information so the reader can better understand my relationship to Source.

My relationship is mine. *Your relationship to Source is* yours. *I can be upset with Source. I can curse at Source. I can cry to Source. I can laugh with Source. I can doubt the existence of Source. I can even argue with Source. But dear reader, please trust and know, that I am loved and favored by Source and so are you, whatever beliefs that you have.*

If you get one thing from reading this book, I hope that you walk away with a better understanding of Source so that you too can build a personal relationship (if you haven't already) with Source.

Past Life Regressionist #1: *Hmm.*

Aliya: So, for the portal, you would have to get a sense one is there. Listen to... I'm seeing intuition, third eye and maybe when I think one is present, to stare at it. Stare and let my eyes see and not have my brain make it into something else. They can't make me see. Even if they showed me the portal, my brain would correct it.

Past Life Regressionist #1: *Hmm*, so...

Aliya: So, it's a learned... It's something learned with the human brain.

Past Life Regressionist #1: So, it takes practice. Okay.

Aliya: *There's nothing to unlock here.*

Training your brain and eyes to perceive portals involves developing your intuitive senses, refining your energetic awareness, and shifting your perception beyond the physical. Your third eye would need to be activated in order to intuitively pick up the changing energy around you. You would also need to perform visualization exercise to help train the brain (and eyes) to recognize subtle shifts in energy. Your sensitivity to energies would need to be strengthened. This can be done by practice seeing auras. Working with strong healers and shamans could also help to attune your energy to nature as well as help you to shift your awareness into a state where portals are more visible.

Past Life Regressionist #1: Okay, how does she know, or can you ask Source, how you know when you are astral projecting?

Aliya: They're showing me a time where I took somebody else with me, so they're just saying... Well, I'm astral projecting. There isn't a question if I'm astral projecting or not, I know I'm astral projecting. I just do. But I do it when my defenses are down. So, I do it when I'm sleeping or when I'm about to go to sleep.

A funny little thing happens when I close my eyes to sleep. My 3D reality drifts away, and my soul is freed to go wherever it wants to go and does whatever it wants to do. One night, a few years ago, I'd energetically connected to an acquaintance in the spirit realm. I was upset with them and during the argument, I'd taken their hand and said something like, "Let's go to The Keeper and see what he has to say about it!" and the next second, we were both in my private, golden room in the Akashic Records, letting The Keeper mediate our argument.

At the time, I didn't understand the monumental feat I'd just done. I also believe this was my first time going to the Akashic Records without someone else taking me or by listening to self-guided hypnosis videos from YouTube to help me get there. It wasn't until I woke the next morning and asked myself, "Wait. Did I do that by myself?" It was then that I fully understood that I could astral project and also that The Keeper was a true friend.

Past Life Regressionist #1: *Hmm*, okay.

Aliya: That's the easiest time for me. I'm not thinking too hard on it.

Past Life Regressionist #1: Okay. Alright. So, can we provide Aliya with extra gifts of mental strength?

Aliya: Yes.

Past Life Regressionist #1: Can we do that now?

Aliya: Yes.

Past Life Regressionist #1: Okay. Can you let me know when you were done?

Aliya: It's done. I don't think anything… <laughter> I think…

Past Life Regressionist #1: Is it some advice you need?

Aliya: No, I think Source thinks I have all the mental strength I need. But it was gonna be a placebo effect. But I caught onto it…

Past Life Regressionist #1: <laughter> Oh, no! Okay. Well. So, you have all the strength you need already.

Aliya: Source said, I need confidence.

Past Life Regressionist #1: Can we provide you with confidence today? Can Source help you with that?

Aliya: Yes.

Past Life Regressionist #1: Can we do that now?

Aliya: Yes, that's done.

Past Life Regressionist #1: Oh, great! Thank you! So, has Meisha, I hope I'm pronouncing that right, have you shared past lives together? And if yes, which ones?

Meisha is my ten-year-old Chow Chow dog.

Aliya: I've been shown me holding her like, as a daughter.

Past Life Regressionist #1: Okay? And any other lives?

Aliya: She's been my animal before.

Past Life Regressionist #1: What animal was she?

Aliya: Seeing another dog. Oh... There was a horse in one of my past lives that I used to dream about, that died and I'm getting shown that horse.

Past Life Regressionist #1: Was that Meisha too?

Aliya: Yeah, she was. She's been with me as other animals, and one time, as a young daughter.

Past Life Regressionist #1: That's nice. Has Jori and Piper shared past lives together? And if yes, which?

Jori is my oldest son, and Piper was his Beagle that passed away many years ago.

Aliya: They were siblings in a different life. I just see two children holding hands.

Past Life Regressionist #1: Any other lives, also?

Aliya: They share lives where they play and have fun.

Past Life Regressionist #1: As friends, or...

Aliya: I'm just getting the picture of just, a whole bunch of laughter, and like playing.

Past Life Regressionist #1: Okay. Are there any more lives that they share together?

Aliya: No.

Past Life Regressionist #1: Has MJ and Ciara shared past lives together, and if so, which ones?

MJ is my son, and Ciara is his pound puppy.

Aliya: Their love is... I just see...just MJ and Ciara, as she is now, as a dog, but just a lot of love. I don't know if they shared lives, or if it's just their connection of love. They have a... I just… I see a line going from them and it's… So, they are connected. I'm just being shown they are connected in love.

Past Life Regressionist #1: Okay. Beautiful. So, can Source help you open up to be more in a receiving energy of especially love, wealth, and abundance.

Aliya: I'm already there. I've been preparing and working on it hard, and Source appreciates that I put in the work, like, I find my faults, and I put in the work myself. Source likes that I'm doing my little meditations, like, I'm making up my own meditations, and I know what I'm lacking, and I fill those holes in myself. Source is saying, I'm where I need to be, like, I'm strong as I need to be. So, like I have everything.

Past Life Regressionist #1: Okay, wow. Can Source help you to become more luckier?

Aliya: Yes.

Past Life Regressionist #1: Can we do it now?

Aliya: Yes, it's done.

Past Life Regressionist #1: Great. So, what is the next step on your journey?

Aliya: I'm just being shown me, and I get a seat at a table, and I'm talking, so I guess… And I'm kinda high up. So, I guess… I'm going to be elevated. I'm gonna be… I'm gonna be seen. I'm gonna be looked at. I'm gonna be… I'm gonna have support. They're showing me… Someone's got their hand on my shoulder, kind of holding me down, grounding me. It's… They're not telling me this, they're showing me something. So, I'm trying to figure out. Like, I'm talking, like, I'm like… I'm on a panel, but it's just me and I'm talking, and people are around listening.

Past Life Regressionist #1: Is this like a live situation thing? Are people live there with you? Would it be more a podcast setting?

Aliya: They're live. Is this a podcast? I… I don't know. That's a good question. I don't know cause… I just… I just see me talking and being animated and…and I know that people are...a bunch of people are listening to me. But I can't see if... I can't... I can't tell that. That's a good point. I don't know.

Past Life Regressionist #1: Can you ask Source to focus more in on what exactly it would be that you are doing?

Aliya: Now, I'm like, on a stage and spotlights are on me.

Past Life Regressionist #1: Are you still sitting at a panel?

Aliya: No. I'm standing up, and it's just me, and I'm talking.

Past Life Regressionist #1: What are you talking about?

Aliya: I'm talking about my life and my path and my journey.

Past Life Regressionist #1: Are you inspiring people with your story? Is that why you're talking on stage?

Aliya: Yeah, I'm telling my story and how I came to be and I'm talking about Source and about what needs... What the collective needs to do.

Past Life Regressionist #1: So, your next step, as I understand it, would be to go more out into the public and let yourself be seen and heard more?

Aliya: Yes. I am doing that. Source is saying that I am doing that already, it's just, that it's gonna be on a larger scale. Eventually.

Past Life Regressionist #1: Can you ask Source, if there is something that you can do now to put that process more into motion of getting there?

Aliya: Be more authentic. I don't have to try hard. I don't have to... I don't have to follow the model of the...of the Tarot card readers or psychics on social media. I watch them a lot, but I don't have to follow their motto. That's for them, it's not... How they gained their success, it's how they were supposed to gain their success. That's not how I will gain mine. But talk about what I feel called to talk about, and that's how I will get the people.

At this point, I had been trying to model them. But realized that didn't feel good, right or authentic to me. Being a psychic and connecting with people spiritually and energetically is my calling, not reading tarot cards on social media.

Past Life Regressionist #1: Okay.

Aliya: Be auth…When I'm not authentic, people can tell. So, just be truly authentic.

Past Life Regressionist #1: Okay. Alright. Is there anything else that Source has as a message for you, or something that we think you need to hear right now?

Aliya: It'll come. I'm fine. Source… They're undoing old ways, and it hurts to have old ways unraveled and new ways built up and I'm doing a fine job at that. It doesn't… It doesn't look like… It doesn't look like how I think it should look because I'm still looking at it with old eyes. That's it.

At this point, the regressionist asks Source if Source has any messages for her. Prior to our session, when reviewing the questions that I had for Source, I'd encouraged the regressionist to ask Source questions regarding her life that she needed answered. Those questions have nothing to do with me, my journey or what needs to be shared with the collective for this book and are very private in nature, so I will not reveal them here. The below is what was said in closing and provided here for closure to this session, as well.

Past Life Regressionist #1: Okay. Well, thank you so much. Thank you to Source and thank you too. So, we are now going to bring your light body back to your physical body and I want all of the consciousness and personality of Aliya to, once again, return and integrate into the body completely. We're just bringing your energy back to your physical form. All of your renewed and realigned and vibrant energy is returning now into your body.

Chapter Nineteen
Aliya
Past Life Regression: 13-NOV-2024

I'd connected to the past life regressionist #2, the same as I had regressionist #1. We were all learning our craft and found that practicing on each other was a great option as it gave us space to learn without fear or judgement. I had done an intuitive psychic reading and a past life regression on regressionist #2 and was repaying the favor by offering my services so she could practice her talents.

Past Life Regressionist #2: You are traveling to the most necessary place. You are traveling to the life with Noatok. You are moving through barriers of where you thought you could not go further. You move through the barriers of where you have never been before and never before imagined you could go and you do, because you can. And you are the very essence of this movement and light. You are finally arriving here and now to the most relevant time, arriving here and now to the most necessary place.

As the movement slows, you begin to gather your barring's and as the movement stops, you begin to feel your point of view. I want you to tell me, the very first thing that you see or the very first impression that you have as you begin to understand where you are and what is happening around you. Tell me, what do you see or feel in this new space?

Aliya: I think I'm standing, like, I'm in, I think, I'm in a jungle and I'm standing on a...the roots of a big tree. Like...they're kind of, the roots are kind of out of the ground and I'm standing on the roots that... I've got my right hand leaning on a tree and it's kind of damp.

Past Life Regressionist #2: And how do you feel in this space as you look around?

Aliya: I'm just wondering where I am.

Past Life Regressionist #2: Okay, and is there anything that stands out the most to you where you are?

Aliya: No, just…there are a lot of trees.

Past Life Regressionist #2: Okay, I want you to look down at your feet. Can you tell me, are you wearing anything on your feet?

Aliya: No, I'm barefoot. And I…

Past Life Regressionist #2: You said one hand was on the tree, but if you look at your other hand, are you carrying anything?

Aliya: At first, I wasn't carrying anything, but I think I have a baby on my hip.

Past Life Regressionist #2: And what are you wearing on your body?

Aliya: *Mmm.* So, I think I'm like, in the Amazon and I'm a native. A native woman. I kind of look Native American, like, long dark hair and just native. So, even my dress. I have on a short skirt and like, a… Like, a band that covers up my chest. And I've got jewelry and like, bindings or something going up my arms. Like, really decorative stuff.

Past Life Regressionist #2: And how do you feel about the baby that's sitting on your hip?

Aliya: It's my baby. It's a baby boy. I think I'm just… He's young, not a… Maybe one or two. And I'm just… I know he's not ready yet but I'm kind of teaching him, like, about connecting and I'm connecting us to this tree, like our energy.

Past Life Regressionist #2: And do you feel younger or older?

Aliya: I'm young.

Past Life Regressionist #2: All right. So, what I would like to do now, is move you to your home or your place of residence. Now, that we understand a little bit about your past self, what I want to do is leave this space and move forward to your place of residence. Your home in the life that we are currently reviewing. This is where you live in the life that we are viewing. One, two, three. We are now moving forward to your place of residence. You are standing outside, in front of your place of residence. Tell me, what do you see? What does the outside of your home look like?

Aliya: Before, I was walking through like, the village with the baby on my hip and it was like, it was just a lot of different voices, children laughing. *Um*, I don't know if I'm... I can't really see... I'm trying to see where I live. I... I... I get the idea that maybe... Like, I really can't see the outside, but I see the inside. It's just like, a dirt floor, very rudimentary, just a small dirt floor. I see like a, like a... I don't... There's a palette off to one side and I know that's where I sleep.

Past Life Regressionist #2: Is there space for your baby inside of the home?

Aliya: No, it's very small, like...I'm kind of in a tent. The baby sleeps with me.

Past Life Regressionist #2: Okay. And...

Aliya: Oh, okay! I see the outside now. It is, like a teepee? It's not white, but kind of off white and it's got like, designs on the outside, like painted designs. The designs aren't really significant. I think someone just... I did it and I was proud to do it. Like, it was, like, it was my first time painting my tent.

Past Life Regressionist #2: Beautiful. And is it just you and the baby that live in the tent together?

Aliya: I feel like a man lives there, too.

Past Life Regressionist #2: So, we are now going to move to the dinner table. On the count of three, we are going to be at the dinner table or on the floor at the dinner. One. Two. Three. You are now sitting down to eat your evening meal. As you sit down, tell me, what is in front of you at the dinner table?

Aliya: It's not a table. We're just sitting in the dirt. It's me and my mate and the baby. We're laughing and we have bread, and me and my mate are talking and laughing, just enjoying each other, sharing bread. But I get the feeling that if we want something more than bread, we would go out and eat with the others, but we're taking some time out by ourselves right now.

Past Life Regressionist #2: Okay, and how do you feel, I know in this moment, it seems a positive feeling towards your mate, but overall, how do you feel about your mate?

Aliya: I love him. He's handsome. *Um*, I think I chose him. I think my dad thinks that he chose him, but I think I manipulated my dad. Not in the bad way, but I know how to sway him, and I chose him. I think my dad's a chief.

Past Life Regressionist #2: And how do you feel about your dad?

Aliya: I love my dad. I think he's a... It's like I see him, like, he's... he's... he's... He's big, at least to me, he's big. He has a big chest. He's older now, but he still has muscle. He's firm, like he holds his face firm. But I know that... I'm just getting a really, really good feeling. Like I, like, I'm getting emotional right now thinking about him because I do love him. And I just think, I just think the world of him. He's firm and a lot of people don't know that he's mushy and he doesn't even like to show me that he's mushy, but he's mushy for me. And that's why I can kind of manipulate him because he doesn't like to... It's like, he, he... It's his word. And so, I have to... I know how to talk to him to make him seem like it's still his word, but make it go in my favor.

Past Life Regressionist #2: And how do you feel about being the chief's daughter? Do you have any roles in the community?

Aliya: I'm trying to think, just trying to see how... I just think, I just have a regular place. I guess we're all just a community. I think I just... I just fall in line, like everyone else.

Past Life Regressionist #2: Alright, so now that we've taken a look at who you are and where you live, we are going to move to your job or occupation. This is where you spend most of your time in the life that we are viewing. We are now moving forward to where you spend most of your time. You are now standing there, tell me, what is happening around you? What do you see?

Aliya: I'm with the other women. The baby is secured to my back, and I am washing clothes. We're just all gathered around, talking and laughing. I'm scrubbing clothes on like, some kind of old-fashioned board or something, just getting the dirt out of clothes.

Past Life Regressionist #2: And are all the women there doing that job or is the washing specifically your job?

Aliya: I think we're all washing our own stuff and we're just all, kind of, meeting here to pass the time. Like, we do chores together because we just… There's just, like, the women are with the women and the men are… I don't know what they're off doing, and I don't know if I care. It's just being with my friends and family.

Past Life Regressionist #2: Alright, so now that we've taken a look at who you are, where you live, and how you spend your time. I want to move you to the most important date in the life that we are currently viewing. This will help us understand why you are being shown this specific life. We are now leaving the space and moving forward to an important day. A day that you consider to be important in the life we are watching. One. Two. Three. You are there now. You are now viewing an important day. Tell me what is happening? What do you see?

Aliya: I think like…chaos. I don't know what's going on. I think people are in the village that aren't supposed to be in the village, and everyone's kind of…running. I don't know if they're setting fire to stuff.

Past Life Regressionist #2: Okay. Let's move backwards and find out what happens. You're going to move backwards to just before this scene, so we can understand what happened. One. Two. Three. You are now, before this scene took place. Tell me what is happening?

Aliya: Everybody is sitting around the fire at night. The men are in the middle and the women are kind of on the outer circle as they're explaining that…talking about a plan or somebody's coming. We're gonna get raided. We know something's coming.

Past Life Regressionist #2: How do they know that?

Aliya: Yeah, I don't know. But for… They're quietly talking and we're, I think we're a little scared. It's just dark and quiet and they're talking, and the women were like, it's…it's the men's job to figure this out, but we are hanging back, not a part of it, but we can listen quietly.

Past Life Regressionist #2: What is the action plan that the men come up with?

Aliya: There's a, I think a bunch of ideas, like to move the women and the children and some men want to go to them and not have it come to us. Some men want to stay and fight and let them come to us. But I get the feeling that we think we have more time than we do because then in the morning, like before we even wake up, they're already there. And so, it seems like we don't have a plan yet, because we thought we had more time.

Past Life Regressionist #2: Okay, and let's move now to the end of the scene. Can you tell me, are you and your family safe?

Aliya: Yes, there's smoke. I think part of our house was burnt and it's smoky and my mate and I have the baby with me. My mate is, like upset in our house. I don't think we lost anyone, is just that, they just… I don't think the idea was to kill us or anything. It's just the idea was to come and teach us a lesson. And so, they are… I don't think we harm each other. I think the idea was just to be disruptive. Cause, like, I see smoke, but I like… It's our village…just saw our village and I don't think anyone is harmed. We're just in shock.

Past Life Regressionist #2: And do you know who these people are that came to raid your village?

Aliya: It's just another tribe. It's just…just another tribe. I get the feeling we don't have much going on <laughing>, but it's just this other tribe and us. That we're just kind of misbehaving and we're just creating issues between each other.

Past Life Regressionist #2: Okay.

Aliya: I'm wondering... It's just like, a little rivalry, but not, not even, *uh*... I'm saying, lighthearted, but they burnt down our village. I don't know if... I don't think these people have like, true cares. Now that I'm like, looking... I'm like...don't think...

Past Life Regressionist #2: Kind of like children fighting?

Past Life Regressionist #2: Yes.

Past Life Regressionist #2: Okay, okay, alright.

Aliya: I think... I don't know why... It has something to do with my mom, though.

Past Life Regressionist #2: Alright. Well, let's lean into that. What do you see or feel about that?

Aliya: Because I didn't really see my mom, but it was, like a lingering energy... And... I think that's my mom's people. And I think she's... I don't know if I should... I don't know, like. I don't know where I'm getting it from, but I think it's my mom. My mom is there and she's important there. I think it's what I want to say. And she's upset with...her and my dad are there... That's very interesting. I think those two are just being bratty.

Past Life Regressionist #2: So, they're part of this rivalry in some way?

Aliya: Yeah, I don't know to the extent. I don't really...

Past Life Regressionist #2: Okay, alright. So, now that we've viewed this important day, we are going to move forward to another important day. Another day, that you feel is important when something is happening. We are now leaving this space and moving forward to an important day. A day that you consider to be important in the life we are watching. You are there now. You are now viewing an important day. Tell me, what do you see? What is happening around you?

Aliya: My mom is in our village. She's talking to my dad and I'm kind of mediating. Noatok is older, not too much, but he's older. And she is demanding to be able to be in his life.

She's kind of haughty. She's a strong... A strong sorcerer shaman. And she's saying that he has the gift and he's stronger than even me *and* her. And she's telling my dad that, *uh*... She's just going to be a part of his life and I'm kind of like, *well, he is* my *son*. And she's telling me, I know that this is the way. So, I think we're just resolving these issues. I think she wanted to raise me a certain way and that's where they disagreed and so, they were just doing this petty rivalry back and forth because of that.

Past Life Regressionist #2: So, the other group that came and raided, that was your mom's family?

Aliya: *Mm hmm.*

Past Life Regressionist #2: And she had that done because she was upset with the way your father was dealing with you and raising you?

Aliya: Not that. I think, if she was upset, she could have come and got me at any time, but she's more...it's their feelings towards each other. They love each other, but they're just, they're just being bratty towards each other.

Past Life Regressionist #2: Okay, and your son is Noatok?

Aliya: Yes.

Past Life Regressionist #2: And you or your mom is aware that he has an important role in all of this?

Aliya: *Mm hmm.*

Past Life Regressionist #2: Okay, and what are your thoughts about him or his powers?

Aliya: To me, he's just a baby.

Past Life Regressionist #2: Okay, beautiful. So, we are going to go to one last important day. Another day that you feel is important when something is happening. You can take us to a day that will help us understand why we're being shown this lifetime. We are now leaving the space and moving forward to an important day. You are there now. You are now viewing one last important day. Tell me what is happening? What do you see?

Aliya: *Um*, I see Noatok and he's coming into his powers. It's just, *uh*... I just see things kind of floating around him. Like, things levitating around him.

Past Life Regressionist #2: So, he's able to make things levitate?

Aliya: Yeah, I think that's when I see like, the full extent of... Like, he's still little, but I'm just getting a glimpse of his potential.

Past Life Regressionist #2: And has anyone taught this to him or is this something he just knows?

Aliya: He just was born into it.

Past Life Regressionist #2: And how do you react to his powers?

Aliya: Like, *oh shit*. Like, this is...cause he's still a baby and he's laughing and he... I don't think he's even aware (of what he's doing). He's just doing it because it makes him laugh. And I realize that I don't know if I've just, I'm just kind of awestruck. I'm just awestruck.

Past Life Regressionist #2: Okay, beautiful, how old is he right now?

Aliya: Four.

Past Life Regressionist #2: Do you ever talk to him about his powers? Did he say anything to you about them?

Aliya: That's why I...that seeing...where I have... I know he's special and I can kind of feel it vibrating from him. And I just make sure that I talk... I'm like...sitting on the rocks and we're feeling the vibration from the rocks and we're just feeling these vibrations of the Earth around us. And I'm just really, just teaching him how to ground into...use the Earth's energy to help him ground and connect with everything. And I like, I don't, I don't know if I do this too? And that's how I know, but I just... I'm hearing, I'm just teaching him the way.

Maybe my mom did this to me. And so, I was just out doing the same thing. We just go off and have our own thing, just the two of us. Our own little lessons where we're just spending time and it's not really just teaching, because I don't think I can teach him anything. I'm just… I'm just exposing him.

Past Life Regressionist #2: Very beautiful. So, what we're going to do now, is we are going to move into the last day of your life, in the life that we are watching. You are now moving forward to the very last day of your life in the life you are currently viewing. You are there now. Tell me as you watch yourself in this new space, what is happening? What do you see?

Aliya: I'm just an old lady, lying down.

Past Life Regressionist #2: Is anyone there with you?

Aliya: I think there are, but I am like already kind of in the light already.

There's a calmness and the feeling of completion. In my mind, all I can see is warm bright light enveloping me. I'm not really concerned or worried about that life anymore. I'm actively leaving it.

Past Life Regressionist #2: Okay, so what became of Noatok and his powers during your lifetime?

Aliya: It was a good life just watching him. I don't, I get the feeling…because I don't know if I ever see him grown. I just have in my head that he's off doing… that he's off doing stuff.

Past Life Regressionist #2: Okay, he left home at a young age?

Aliya: That's not it either. I think he like, I know that he goes through portals, like he leaves. Like, he leaves, and he comes back. So, I know he's not bound to that time.

My short theory here is that the little boy that the clients see during their regressions, is this same little boy from this time period. He's a powerful being that's not constricted to human limitations. This little boy, this magical little boy, heard an energetic variation of his mother crying and calling out for help and answered the call. This child is moving through the spiritual realm with knowledge and free will and he is not bound to this 3D world or the constraints of it. He comes and goes as he pleases.

Aliya Griffin

Chapter Twenty

Past Life Regressionist #2: Okay, interesting. And so, as you are going into the light, can you describe to me what this process looks like and where you go from here?

Aliya: Right now, I think I'm just... I'm just like, in a space of just light and content, and I'm just...content.

Past Life Regressionist #2: Okay, alright. Do you look... Do you have the ability to look back at the life that you just came from?

Aliya: If I... If I wanted to do that, I could go and talk to the council. Like, right now, I'm just... Like, relaxing in the light.

Past Life Regressionist #2: Okay, alright, so what we will do is we will now go to Source. Does that feel good for you?

Aliya Yes.

Past Life Regressionist #2: Okay, so now that we've looked back at the life that we just came from, what I want you to do is move forward and introduce or reacquaint you with Source, God, whatever you call this energy, itself. On the count of three, you are going to find yourself in the direct presence of Source. One. Two. Three. You are now present with Source. Tell me, do you feel the energy of Source present in this new space?

Aliya: Yes.

Past Life Regressionist #2: What does it feel like in the space?

Aliya: I'm anxious, a little nervous, but...it's a good kind and like, excited, too.

Past Life Regressionist #2: Okay, so let's ask Source for some light to help release that anxious and nervous feeling, so that you can be fully present there without it. And let's connect with Source to see if Source has any words of wisdom for you. I am now calling forward Source, God, Creator. May we please speak with Source? May we please speak with Source?

Aliya: *Yes.*

Past Life Regressionist #2: Do we have permission to ask questions from Source?

Aliya: *Yes.*

Past Life Regressionist #2: Okay, wonderful, thank you. Can you tell us the purpose of why that life that we just viewed was brought forward?

Aliya: *She wanted to see the life with Noatok.*

Past Life Regressionist #2: Okay, alright, and can we please bring Noatok forward to join us in this meeting space so we can discuss Aliya's future?

Aliya: *Yes, he's here.*

Past Life Regressionist #2: Okay, wonderful. What should Aliya be doing that she's not already doing to help her on her journey?

Aliya: *She's stressed even though...even though we've told her how it's gonna happen and guided her, she still remains stressed. There's nothing...nothing needs to be done. It's just... It's gonna happen.*

Past Life Regressionist #2: What can we do today to help her with that stress? Can we send Source's healing light, or is there anything else we can do today?

Aliya: *She has the ability to call on Source and help with this. It's just that...we can... We can do it. It's just gonna come back.*

Past Life Regressionist #2: Alright, what can we do to help with the stress so that it doesn't keep coming back?

Aliya: *It's just gonna keep coming back as she takes... As she moves forward, she... Something in her gets really afraid of leaving the old life behind, so she tries to reach back to grab some of it. It's just a process.*

Past Life Regressionist #2: Do you have any suggestions for her as she does this to help her with the process?

Aliya: *No, it's just a process she has to move through.*

Past Life Regressionist #2: Okay, can you explain Noatok's relationship to Aliya?

Aliya: *It was already explained to her, she just... Likes to hear things again.* <laughter>

Past Life Regressionist #2: Okay, so let's tell her again.

Source and my spirit team have told me over and over again that everything will work out and they have a plan for me. But in my defense, life is hard, and it makes me feel good to have Source reassure me that I'm fine. So, many thanks to this regressionist who knew how important it was for me to receive additional reassurance.

Aliya: *Noatok is her child born out of love. Purest love. Not every... Not, not all souls strive to do this, and not all can.* He's, *um*, but he's too powerful to be, *um*, to have, *uh*, a reincarnation because of who and what he is. So, he doesn't hold human forms...and that life we led... He wanted to come through, but he didn't stay long. There's no way. There's no way.

This topic needs to be explored a bit more because Client B saw his energy as her son (young, then older) in her past life. I'm unsure if he was able to hold that human form because he'd finally mastered it or if (as suspected) he was able to come through because he'd used a fraction of his energy. This exploration is for another book, as I continue to learn about Noatok.

Past Life Regressionist #2: So, when you said not all souls are able to do this, are you referring to give birth out of true love or you're referring to Noatok's capabilities?

Aliya: *No, not... The goal of soul is to keep learning, keep experiencing and bring it back to the collective so that we all know. So, the goal is not... Like the humans have... The goal is to get married, have children, have a legacy. The Souls understand that their knowledge and their experiences is their legacy. So, there's no need to have children to build up a legacy, because the legacy is infinite. It's infinity. It goes on and on and on.*

So, for Souls, there is no need to have children. That's just not like, that's not... That's a human thing. So, for the Souls... If a Soul is old enough and has learned most of the experiences that it needs to learn... Because there is no way to learn all the experiences. It's...it's...every...every second, every breath brings a new...something new to learn. So, there is no way to learn everything.

But a Soul who has ascended really high, and who does know most of it, they have a choice. And one of the choices is to...experience this... I was gonna say ultimate love, but it's not even ultimate love. It's... I'm trying to look for the word. I'm just gonna use ultimate, because that's, I think the only thing I know like, a human way to describe it. But Source is the ultimate, ultimate love, but it's a different word. I don't know. I don't know.

Past Life Regressionist #2: Unlimited or...?

Aliya: *I don't know.*

Past Life Regressionist #2: Okay.

Aliya: *I'm gonna say, ultimate, but... So, in order to just... Oh, I can just say... Oh, for another experience. So, because that's one thing that Souls don't strive to do, is have children. That's just not... That's just not thought about. But if you ascend high, and you have mastered, then you are given a choice, and it's not even open to everyone, but you are given a choice to ascend even higher than the highest of high. And that would be to experience bringing forth...birthing a, putting quotation marks,* "birthing a Soul from two Souls." So, two Souls don't birth Souls. Souls all come from Source.

Past Life Regressionist #2: Okay.

Aliya: *But that's what Noatok is. Her and her soulmate decided that they…their love for each other is so strong that they wanted to create something together. So, they created Noatok, and Noatok has a sister, so they have twins that they created. And so, these twin Souls are outside of the…outside of the normal Soul.* I'm seeing, like, a sphere. *So, the… So, these Soul babies, and there's not a lot, live out…* Like, I see… Like, a little… Most of the Souls are in this sphere, and a few are outside of this sphere, kind of ping ponging. So, they don't… They don't follow normal rules. There are different rules for them.

As you might can tell from this passage above. I'm exhibiting signs of fatigue (having trouble holding my words and thoughts). Although my body is comfortable in my bed, my soul is with Source and Noatok, which are both pretty heavy and the experience is energetically draining.

Past Life Regressionist #2: Okay, so if there's, if most souls come directly from Source, and these souls… What would be a good name for these souls?

Aliya: *Hmm They are still Souls, Aliya, just calls them soul babies.*

Past Life Regressionist #2: Okay, so if most souls come from Source and these souls are created—

Aliya: *They all come… They all come from Source. They're still from Source.*

Past Life Regressionist #2: Right.

Aliya: *It's just that instead of Source making them, the two Souls made them. But since the two Souls are Source…*

Past Life Regressionist #2: So, those two souls have to be pretty evolved as you…in order to…

Aliya: *Yes.*

Past Life Regressionist #2: Okay, wow, that's fascinating. Okay, okay, so how can Aliya best utilize Noatok's help?

Aliya: I'm just hearing, *call on him. He's, he's not here to do anything. He's just here because she needs the extra love and support. And he is her son, and it's hard to keep a son away from a hurting mother.*

Past Life Regressionist #2: What lessons does she still need to learn for this current transition?

Aliya: *Her hardest lesson right now is to let go and to be patient and trust, but she knows all this and it's hard for her. I don't think she is going to ever just be able to release control because she knows a lot and she's lived many lives, and that's the…it's one of the… it's… What word is that? It's…it's one of the side effects of living so many lives. It's hard to release control and to let things unfold as they should, because she knows how they* should *unfold, but she just kind of wants to get through it really fast.*

Past Life Regressionist #2: Okay, well, when you say she's…you don't see her ever doing that. Can you expand on that? Because is that not something that she should have as a goal?

Aliya: *The goal isn't to never… It's to… It's to… The goal isn't to get to a place where she doesn't worry about anything, she doesn't stress about anything, she doesn't… She's already released that. That isn't the goal. She's meant to stress. She's meant to worry. She's meant to hold on tight. Um… Because she's meant to experience life, and that's all experiences, and that gets…* I'm seeing, that… It gets my adrenaline going, it gets my ideas flowing, it puts me in a different state of vibration, so all these things are supposed to happen, and then I, *um*, then I deal with it. And I learn how to deal with it, and then I move on to the next problem. But I just see me like, kind of ascending with each…with each bout of worry.

Past Life Regressionist #2: Okay, so the goal is to try to let go as much as possible, but then the next time there will be something else to let go of, and it will be constant.

Aliya: Yeah, it's just so... It's so... So, what I've... I'm having a hard time talking... So, so what I learned before, this is Aliya talking, what I learned before, is that my lesson this time is patience and letting go.

Before, I was channeling Source. I wanted to be clear that it was me talking and not Source, so that I could provide an explanation to the regressionist.

It's hard for me to explain channeling, but I'll do my best. When I'm channeling, it feels like I'm stepping aside—I'm still here, but I'm not the one talking or forming the thoughts. I don't have to force it; I just let it happen. It's a bit like dreaming while awake, except it's clearer, and there's this undeniable sense of wisdom and rightness. The words from my mouth feel true. My brain isn't blank. It's beyond blank. I can't feel it. I'm outside of it.

The slip from me being aware of myself, to me realizing that I'm channeling is pretty seamless. So seamless that I've probably already been channeling for a few minutes before I realize that I'm channeling. The words I'm speaking aren't mine because I have no thought behind the words, they're just coming, and my mouth is moving.

If I'm in a psychic reading session, I'm able to relay a small message from me to the Client, at the start of it. Usually, that message is, "I'm channeling, and the information needs to get out. I'm not trying to be rude, but I am gonna talk over you." Or, I do what I did here, I ask the client to remember something for me (usually the last thought I had before the channel began) and remind me of it later. Even the last thought that I had before the channeling began is elusive.

Think of it like a computer buffering a video from the internet. The video player downloads and temporarily stores a portion of the video ahead of what's currently being watched. If there's a disruption of the internet, the video player will continue to play the part of the video that was temporarily stored before it stops. The video player doesn't have any information to continue playing the video and you have to wait until the connection resumes to continue.

Past Life Regressionist #2: Okay.

Aliya: So, I used to try to practice patience and letting go and try not to be in a position where I had to let something go or where I had to be impatient about something because I was really upset that I wasn't learning patience and letting go. And so, what I learned from a different download, was that...that wasn't something I'm supposed to free myself of. The whole life...the whole life is to learn patience and letting go.

I will always be presented with scenarios where I have to learn how to let go or to be patient. So, that is the theme. And then after the life is over, I have learned the lesson. When I'm reviewing my life, I can look back at all the times where I had to let go or where I had to practice patience. So, it's a theme throughout. I'm not... I'm not ever gonna get *over* it. There will always be times where I have to learn how to let go of something or to be patient.

Past Life Regressionist #2: Alright, got it. Okay, so we're gonna go back to asking Source questions. Okay? Does Aliya have any important responsibilities when she's not incarnated? And what are they? Like, does she have any jobs, etc.?

Aliya: *She thinks, she works at the Akashic Records.*

Past Life Regressionist #2: Okay, when you say, "she thinks", is that correct or not correct?

Aliya: *I mean... She can... I have no control over what jobs they decide to do.*

Past Life Regressionist #2: Okay, okay, anything else besides the Akashic Records?

Aliya: *At that point in time, when she was shown that, that's what she did.*

Past Life Regressionist #2: Okay. Where does Source originate from?

Aliya: Everywhere, I just see like, a spark in the dark. Like, a lonely spark of nothingness, and then a full consciousness and then this…this idea to create and to expand and keep creating and keep expanding.

Past Life Regressionist #2: Right. How did humans on Earth come to be?

Aliya: *Mmm.* Just a minute, I'm trying to get stuff… I'm getting like a… I don't know if… It's like a vision of seeds being planted, but not, like in the ground. Like, it's a… It's kind of weird, like a group effort. Like, a, *um*… I'm just trying to see it. It's like, *um*… there's Earth, it's like, you know, beautiful, it's clean, it's new, and it's like… Like, I try… Like I'm seeing stuff from the like, I don't even know, from outside of Earth… Like kind of just…

Okay, I'm just gonna explain it because I can't make sense of it. But I see like, huge hands like, planting people here. But it's not just one set of hands. It's a few different sets of hands planting people here. And Source is just like, okay, that's fine. If that's what you want to do…saying that to the people that are planting. But I'm also getting that the people that planted original humans here, they were different than the humans today. (Humans today) have been so genetically modified by the environment, that we are much different from when we were first planted here. It doesn't make sense to me.

Past Life Regressionist #2: What did we look like when we were first planted here? Or what were the differences rather?

Aliya: We were cleaner and healthier. We knew who we were. We knew the rules. We had more harmony and there wasn't a whole bunch of us. We were put here to just, like, inhabit this new planet, like, *uh*, but it's, but it got, it got polluted. I'm just seeing, like it, like as the planet got polluted… So, oh, okay, so the…the humans were here. Divine beings here started off like, an… Oh, okay, I'm getting a lot.

So, this wasn't the only place that, you know, beings were put to live. You know, because the whole idea is to grow and expand and learn. Grow and expand and learn. This wasn't the, the only planet. There are different and more. Source is saying, not to go into all that. But there are more. And how species develops is reflective on how they… I'm seeing a ping pong. The species is related to the planet, and the planet is related to the species. If the planet is pure and nice, that's what the species is.

And then as they evolve… I'm seeing, like, the core of the Earth. If it's neglected… If Earth is neglected, if things aren't being taken care of, I'm just seeing, like, grainy. I don't know, I'm just trying to explain like this graininess that I'm seeing. Then that, just pollution, I guess is the word I'm looking for, pollution. Then the pollution then affects, then it's like a mirror. Oh, it's like a mirror. So, if the people are all being polluted, that pollutes the planet, and then that reflects back on the people, and the people are further polluted. I think I'm going in circles now.

Past Life Regressionist #2: No, that makes sense. It's a cycle and you're describing a cycle. Good, thank you for that. What is the purpose of Earth?

Aliya: *The purpose of Earth like all the other planets are for creation and beauty and life.*

Past Life Regressionist #2: When this human experience of Aliya is completed, and she returns home in the spirit realm, how long would she have been gone from the spirit realm?

Aliya: It's blank.

Past Life Regressionist #2: Okay. Because there is no time in the spirit realm?

Aliya: *Yeah. It's just she goes, she goes back there and it's hard for her to understand, because she goes back and she knows that she's not there and she's only coming back, but then it's, like, it's a blank…and that confuses her, because she doesn't understand that time really is just… It's… It's nothingness. So, if her loved ones think that she's only gone for a blink then she's only gone for a blink. And if she goes back and they see her and they talk to her, then they're able to hold space for that because there is no, there is no time. It's confusing and I can't get into it, because it'll just confuse... But it's just a...no time at all.*

On one of my solo and personal visits to the Akashic Records, I'd asked The Keeper to explain time to me. While there, his explanation made perfect sense, but when I tried bringing that knowledge and information back to the 3D world with me, I couldn't explain it properly because my human brain couldn't wrap around the terms, ideas, etc. and basically, it was driving me crazy. I was shown a deck of playing cards. He spread out the cards, end to end, stating, that is how humans perceive time, as linear. Then he restacked the cards, so they were on top of each other and pointed a laser at the top card on the deck. The laser went through the middle of all the cards. He explained that everything can exist at the same time across realms and time is not linear. In a different book, I'll write about my times visiting the Akashic Records and my time with The Keeper there.

Past Life Regressionist #2: Okay, got it. And how many members are in Aliya's soul family?

Aliya: First, I saw twenty-seven, now I'm seeing thirty-two.

Past Life Regressionist #2: And how many of those have reincarnated on Earth with her for this life? And who are they? And please provide their Earthly names.

Aliya: *She knows the ones that she's seen so far. So, Margie got activated...and she knows Reece and Thella and Kyrstina and Mia...Myles, Jori... Mike.*

I've known my siblings; Reece and Thella were my soulmates. When I was a teenager, I'd previously seen a past life that I'd shared with them. A year prior to writing this book, I'd learned my daughter, Mia and niece, Kyrstina, were part of my soul family. This was the first time I'd learned of the others mentioned here.

Past Life Regressionist #2: Are there any that she has yet to meet?

Aliya: *Yes, she has a soul... The second half of her. The family that's here with her are rushing towards her now. She's... The terminology that she's using is, soul tribe.*

Past Life Regressionist #2: Okay, will you provide any of those names now?

Aliya: *No.*

Past Life Regressionist #2: Okay. Is Aliya—

Aliya: *She will... She will know.*

Past Life Regressionist #2: Is Aliya energetically connected to Rainbow Dancer? And why?

Aliya: *Still energetic...energetically connected to him.* Because, I'm hearing that he's bored. *That she connected with him, and now he knows her energetically, and he doesn't know that many other souls energetically, and so he doesn't interfere, but he... He just likes to watch.*

Past Life Regressionist #2: Does it all negatively affect Aliya in any way?

Aliya: *No, he's just curious.*

During an intuitive psychic reading, I'd met a wonderful young lady from Belgium, and through her, connected to (what we thought at the time) a dragon from another realm. Through this connection, we learned that the dragon, Rainbow Dancer, followed my client from life to life. When I gained more experience doing past life regressions, I'd reached out to her to see if she'd be willing to let me practice on her. Our past life regression session was mind blowing to say the least. Rainbow Dancer wasn't really a dragon, but a Creator God who my client, during one of her past lives, had fallen into (he is a living portal).

As a medium/channel, I still sometimes feel Rainbow Dancer peeking into my life. Not meddling, just observing, like I'm a television show he's watching. He'd previously stated to my client and myself that he enjoyed experiencing things through her eyes because as a Creator God, he creates and doesn't get to see the results of his creations.

I'd wanted to confirm the presence I felt was him, and although I didn't feel anything negative related to our connection, I wanted to make sure that I was fine energetically as Rainbow Dancer is very powerful and energetically heavy. Too heavy for my human mind and body to hold (YouTube: @TheSpiritualGirlie, Past Life Regression 12-SEP-2024).

Past Life Regressionist #2: Okay, what are angels?

Aliya: *Angels are Divine beings. Aliens…*

Past Life Regressionist #2: And what are demons?

Aliya Griffin

Chapter Twenty-One

Aliya: *The same. Humans just like to, um...*

Past Life Regressionist #2: Humanize?

Aliya: *Yeah... humans just like to...* I don't know why I'm so slow now.

The slowness and trouble talking I'd begin experiencing is a normal occurrence during past life regressions. Especially, during a session as energetically heavy as this one.

But humans...humans like to...It's part of the pollution. Instead of owning their own emotions and thought patterns, they like to assign these emotions to outside forces. And they like to assign, the good and the bad, instead of just duality in everything, they like to separate it. And so, they've separated angels as good and demons as bad, when neither is true.

Past Life Regressionist #2: Does Aliya have any angel guides, and if yes, what are their names?

Aliya: *Ezekial, Raphael, and Gabriel. But those are just...* I'm hearing, energetic concepts.

Past Life Regressionist #2: Are they connected to her personally?

Aliya: *Yes, but...yes.*

I've always thought angels were aliens who came to Earth and because, during that time, aliens weren't a thing (Maybe? Or maybe not?) the only way the earlier humans could describe them as, were as angelic beings. But with Source calling them energetic concepts, I need to delve into that explanation further.

"Energetic concepts" likely means that the angels aren't individual beings in the way we typically imagine but rather powerful, divine energies or archetypes that we can connect with, like Noatok.

Each of these angels carries a specific frequency or vibration:
- *Ezekiel is often associated with transformation, visions, and spiritual awakening.*
- *Raphael embodies healing, both physical and emotional.*
- *Gabriel represents communication, divine messages, and clarity.*

Instead of perceiving them as external figures, you might experience them as different aspects of divine energy that guide and support you in your spiritual journey. They could manifest as intuitive insights, healing experiences, or moments of deep inner knowing.

Past Life Regressionist #2: Okay, why is Aliya having such a hard time shedding the thought process from her old life? She wants to step into her full power and embrace her transformation, but she's stuck thinking that she's a regular human and not a creator being.

Aliya: *She knows this, and she understands it very well. The problem is, is that she's having a hard time letting go of her human teachings because it's again, polluted. And so, she has to fight through it. And humans are taught that anything...that anything... They're taught that their true being, their true nature, which is pure and Divine and makes them unique, that if they view themselves as pure and Divine and unique, that something is wrong.*

They are like sheep, cattle taught that they are a... That they, that they are not special, that there's nothing great about them, that there are rules in this human world that need to be followed and they are conditioned that to go outside those human rules would be wrong and make them not right and there are things put in place to scare them away from thinking outside of what they've been taught.

So, if you are psychic, or if you can do things with your mind, or if you could see things, or if you could transcend and ascend, they teach you, speaking of it, believing it, practicing it, will lead to trouble, which is institutionalization. So, they shut up and they be quiet and they stay in line, which is a very low vibration, built off fear and confusion.

She knows she's different and she knows what she can see, and she knows what she can do and she's happy there. But then, it's just the human teachings and pollution gets in the way, and she gets scared, again. So, it's just a...it's just a concept that in time, not right now, and she needs to continue to be gentle with herself, in time, she will be able to shed this. But she also has to understand that she hasn't even been doing this a year and she's a lot further than a lot of, a lot of people. And we're pushing her further and faster. And so, we understand that it's a crash course and it's hard, but she is Iman, and she can do this.

Iman is my Soul's name.

Past Life Regressionist #2: Does Source have any last messages for Aliya or anything that was not asked in her questions that would be helpful for her to know at this stage?

Aliya: I'm getting...*uh* emotional right now because I needed to hear all of that. But Source is saying, I need to practice my breathing. Remember to relax. I am just on the ride, so just trust in it and I'll be where I'm supposed to be.

Past Life Regressionist #2: Beautiful. Does Source have any messages for me before we continue on?

Although, this was a private question the regressionist had for Source, I left it in because the advice given was for the regressionist and myself, and appropriate for sharing.

Aliya: *You are on a similar journey, just of learning and exploration. Like Aliya, you both are just so wound up and tight.* And I just see us like as a ball of paper and like a big hand just like, trying to smooth it out. The wrinkles are always gonna be there, because those wrinkles have been there a long time. So, we're never gonna be, like, fully flat.

I'm just (energetically) reading that to mean that we have life experiences that are never just gonna go away. And that's not the point cause if Source wanted to, Source could (take all of our hardships and pain away). I see, like, an iron. Ironing (the crumpled paper) smooth, but it's not, it's just a hand. So, it's... We're meant to know all that, because that's the experiences we're gonna take with us. We don't understand that now. So, the wrinkles, the life experiences are good. We're meant to experience that. I'm hearing, those are beautiful.

And that will help the collective. That will help everybody going forward. But the goal is just to be able to... I'm just getting, like, stretch and let go and just be. Just be with all those wrinkles in place. But we're not wound...we're not wound any more, we're flat, but we're still wrinkled. But those are getting smoothed out.

Past Life Regressionist #2: Beautiful. I would like to thank Source for all the information and help that Source has given us today. And we are now going to move forward in time and space. Allowing the entity to recede back. The entity from the past life, to recede back to the time and space where they belong, with much love and thanks for the help and information they've given us today. And I would also like to allow Source to recede back into time and space where they belong, with much love and thanks for the help and information they've given us today. And now... we... one moment please... We are going to move forward through time and space to the Akashic Records. In order to be admitted, we must follow and verbally agree to two rules. Rule number one, we cannot look at anyone else's record but our own. Do you agree?

Aliya: Yes.

Past Life Regressionist #2: Rule number two, we must understand the knowledge we seek must be for the good of all and cause harm to none. Do you agree?

Aliya: Yes.

Although, I can go to the Akashic Records without verbally agreeing to these rules, I think it's important, that when I am with someone else (client or regressionist) that we state the rules.

Past Life Regressionist #2: Wonderful. On the count of three, you will find yourself standing in front of the Akashic Records Library. One. Two. Three. You are now standing in front of the Akashic Records Library. Tell me, what do you see in this space?

Aliya: So, I'm in a... I'm in my room. I have a room I go to. So, I'm there already.

In the summer of 2023, during my personal past life regression, I was taken to the Akashic Records Library for the very first time. I arrived in a room. It was like one of the private rooms you would find in a library, but I knew that somehow this was my *private room. It wasn't big, just big enough for a square table that would seat four, two chairs on each side. The walls, however, were beautiful. They were lined in gold with beautiful fixtures and design. This room screamed expensive. It felt luxurious. Even though I've described it in terms of finance, it wasn't, but I can't think of any other words to describe how very valuable and treasured this space felt.*

When I arrived in the room, I saw a big, old and very dusty, leatherbound book on the table. My Akashic Records book that held the story of my soul. Already awe struck by what I was experiencing, things took another turn when the door opened. A male poked his head in and asked, "What are you doing here?" I replied, "To see my book." Or something like that. The male was tall, thin, cloaked in a hood, and I couldn't see his face. I wasn't afraid. I was mostly confused, but immediately it felt that I knew who this figure was. My friend.

I asked him (with the prompting of the regressionist) if he could help me on my journey and he laughed and said, "I'm not getting involved in this." And left. This male energy has appeared every time I've gone to the Akashic Records for myself. During my visits, we often sit in counsel, he gives me advice on life, he holds me while I cry about some human experience or another, or he's openly laughing or teasing me about my humanness.

I hold this energy close and dear to my heart. We are friends now because we're friends across time. I know this and feel this. Once, I asked him if I was loved there (the spiritual realm) and his exact words were, "You are loved, because you are love." These words ring true in my heart, and I repeat this saying whenever I feel lonely.

Past Life Regressionist #2: And can you describe it to me?

Aliya: It's a private room. It's gold everywhere and on this wooden table. I have my book that's waiting for me.

Past Life Regressionist #2: Okay. And can you tell me what that book looks like?

Aliya: It used to be brown leather. Now, for some reason it's kind of coming through as gold, too.

Past Life Regressionist #2: I want you to grab that book and go sit down at the table so we can look into your book and explore your records. Now, that you have your book, what does it feel like in your hands?

Aliya: *Um.* Now it's kind of feeling cold. I think because of the gold. I don't know why it's in gold all of a sudden.

The transformation of an Akashic Record's book from brown leather to gold is a significant and symbolic shift. It could mean a number of different things. Gold often represents higher consciousness, enlightenment, and divine connection. This change could signify that I've reached a new level of spiritual awareness or ascension, where my soul's wisdom and light are more radiant and accessible. My book now being gold could also symbolize great value and importance. It may reflect that I'm fully stepping into my soul's purpose, aligning with my highest path, and embodying my unique spiritual gifts.

The shift to gold also could indicate my vibrational frequency has increased. Gold is associated with purity, abundance, and divine love, suggesting that I'm operating at a higher energetic state. My gold book could mean that my connection to the Akashic Records may be deepening, allowing me to access more profound and expansive wisdom. The golden book could signify mastery over my soul's journey and greater ease in channeling universal truths. The change might also symbolize that I'm now embracing my divine worth and the infinite value of my soul's experiences. It's a reflection of my spiritual achievements and how I'm now honoring my journey.

Past Life Regressionist #2: Alright. So, what we are going to do is, we are going to open up this book and we are going to look for the life that Aliya has led in the future. From the life that she is currently living. Can you open up to a page like that, please?

Aliya: Okay. I have it on the page. But it's kind of blank.

Past Life Regressionist #2: As you look at that page. Does anything start to appear on the page?

Aliya: Horses come to mind?

Past Life Regressionist #2: Is there anywhere on the page that you might see a picture or even just a frame?

Aliya: *Mmm.* I just see horses running.

Past Life Regressionist #2: Okay. Alright. And can you see where the horses are running too?

Aliya: So, I went inside the page.

"Went inside the page." Means that I've energetically leaned in and went through the portal and directly into the life displayed on the page.

I'm just trying to see where I am. For some reason it looks like a sunset and there's two horses running free. I was thinking I was on a beach, but I'm not sure now.

Past Life Regressionist #2: Alright. Well. What do you feel under your feet?

Aliya: First it was sand. Now, I'm getting, maybe I'm still on the beach. It was part sand, but now it's kind of sand and seaweed and dirt.

Past Life Regressionist #2: And as you look down at your body. Can you describe what your body looks like?

Aliya: Think I'm a man. I have on jeans.

What I'm seeing but not describing to the regressionist, is a middle-aged White man with brown hair. Maybe 5'10ish with a stocky build. I have on jeans, but they're rolled up at the cuffs and I'm shirtless.

Past Life Regressionist #2: And if you look down at your hands, are you holding anything in your hands?

Aliya: Like, a stick in one. In my right hand there's a stick. Like, I was walking on the beach, and I just had that stick in my hand.

Past Life Regressionist #2: Let's move forward to see where you are going. Is there any more specific that you're heading?

Aliya: No. I think, I'm just... I think it's just like a little evening stroll, time to myself, walking.

Past Life Regressionist #2: Okay. Alright. So, let's move forward to an important day in that life. A day that will help us understand why this life has come forward and if this life is in the future of Aliya's life right now. One. Two. Three. We have now moved to an important day in this life. Tell me what do you see?

Aliya: A word, *merger*. I like... I have a suit on and it's like, a meeting. It's like, a merger meeting or something. It's a big deal.

Past Life Regressionist #2: And what's your position in this meeting?

Aliya: I'm running it. I'm like, making the deal go through.

Past Life Regressionist #2: And was this meeting successful? We look at the end of the scene.

Aliya: Yeah. I see everybody shaking hands. They're shaking my hand. And I'm shaking people's hands.

Past Life Regressionist #2: Okay. And how are you feeling in this moment?

Aliya: *Um.* Like, good. Good that I was able to get it done.

Past Life Regressionist #2: Alright. Well, let's move forward to another important day. A day in which will help us understand why this life has come forward. One. Two. Three. You are there now, tell me what do you see? What is happening around you?

Aliya: <Shocked> So, I'm looking out my office window and I see the alien ships in the sky.

Past Life Regressionist #2: And how do you feel about the alien ships?

Aliya: I'm going, *"What the hell?"*

Past Life Regressionist #2: Okay.

Aliya: I think everybody. Like, the whole office is abuzz. Like, buzzing. I'm like... In the high rise and I... Like, I'm thinking, because it's more than one, and I'm thinking, I should... I don't know what to do. Like, would there be time to run home to get my family? Like, I am at a loss. Like... To... Like, all the options that are going through my head... I think, I don't know what to do.

Past Life Regressionist #2: And do you know what year it is right now?

Aliya: I'm seeing if I can see a calendar... I see August twenty-seventh on the calendar.

Past Life Regressionist #2: Can you close the calendar and see if there's a year at the front of the calendar?

Aliya: *Um.* So, I don't trust myself, because I did a reading (past life regression session) on someone, and she said that there was going to be an alien invasion in 2072 *(YouTube: @TheSpiritualGirlie, Past Life Regression 25-AUG-2024).*

Past Life Regressionist #2: Okay.

Aliya: So, that's what I'm seeing. But I don't trust that's really me or if that's just a memory I'm grabbing to fill in a space.

Past Life Regressionist #2: That's fine. Well, either way. We'll just go with the August twenty-seven.

Aliya: I see, like, the small 'AUG' and the big, two-seven on the desk calendar. I don't know if I flip... It might be a couple of days past that. I get the idea that I don't do it every day. Like, flipping the calendar isn't something I do every day.

Past Life Regressionist #2: Okay. So, how do you feel about finding someone around you to ask what year it is? Just for reassurance.

Aliya: Right now, we're all really... We're just stuck looking out the window.

Past Life Regressionist #2: It's too chaotic.

Aliya: Yeah. I don't... I'm not near anyone. I can just see from the other office buildings. It's total pandemonium. Because they came from... It's... They came from...and they look black. They just appeared. It's like... It's...it's like... Like, three for sure. Maybe some other ones flying (around the larger ones)?

Past Life Regressionist #2: What do they seem to be doing?

Aliya: They just appeared. It looks very, like... It's like, a nice day out. Like, no clouds and then, there they just are. Just sitting... And what's eerie, is that they're just *sitting* there. Like... I thought they don't even look real.

Past Life Regressionist #2: They're just kind of hovering in the air?

Aliya: *Unmoving.*

Past Life Regressionist #2: *Hmm.* Okay. Alright. So, let's move along to one more important day in the life that you are viewing. We are there now. What is happening around you?

Aliya: Just trying to see... We don't know what's going on. I think it's a meeting and we're trying to figure out what's going on. Someone is saying that we're being rounded up. But I don't know how true that is, if we're being rounded up. But that is what we're all afraid about. And so that's what's really on my mind, is we're being rounded up. But I don't know how... I don't know how... I don't know if that's true, though. But it's just a... I'm standing around like everybody else and we're just trying to figure out what's going on.

Past Life Regressionist #2: And this is still on the same day, when they appear?

Aliya: It's a different day.

Past Life Regressionist #2: Okay. So, what are they doing now? Are they still hovering midair or have they moved?

Aliya: Let me see if I can go to a window. It's so dark out. It's so eerie. Oh, yeah, I look up. I see the moon is shining, giving me light and I just see them. It's just the three.

Past Life Regressionist #2: And you're in the office at nighttime?

Aliya: No, I'm not. I'm like at some kind of community…

Past Life Regressionist #2: Oh. Okay. Got it. Okay. And so, does everybody have a plan of what they're going to do or is everyone just kind of waiting to see what happens?

Aliya: I think everyone's just waiting. The government is not really telling us much. There's nobody outside on the street. It's like, a yellowish glow out there. It's very quiet out there. I think… I think they've been here for some days and now everyone's kind of…they were hiding because there's really nowhere to run. Not like the movies where people just are running. I think there's enough ships in the air, where we know, "Where would we go?"

But they've been just sitting there and it, kind of, someone's saying, like, there's… There's crazy talk is what I'm hearing, and someone's saying that this is the matrix, said they've always been there, but now we can finally see them or those are props and this is all a fake world. Like, everybody's, like… There's confusion around and no one knows, because they are just sitting there, and they look eerie and they're unmoving.

I just had a thought like, why isn't the government moving them? When I look up, I don't see government planes or… Oh, I think maybe the other planes that I saw flying around are us (the government). But for some reason we can't get close to them.

I don't know if I want to see this life. <laughter> This is making me, like, anxious. I don't know.

Chapter Twenty-Two

Past Life Regressionist #2: Just so you know, you are protected. You will not be harmed in any way. Okay? Do you guys see any aliens?

Aliya: <laughing> Not at this point!

Past Life Regressionist #2: Alright. Why don't we... Would you like to recede from this life?

Aliya: Yes! <laughing>

As I started feeling really anxious, Source asked me, "Why are you focusing on a life that's making you anxious when you don't have to?" I realized I wasn't gaining anything from seeing this life. Unlike my past life regressions, where the events had already happened, this one was different—it was a future life. That's why I felt anxious. This future hadn't happened yet in my current timeline, which meant these events were still to come, not something stored safely in the past.

Past Life Regressionist #2: Okay. Let's go back out. You'll be sitting in the Akashic Records.

Aliya: I just... Cause, I just didn't want it. I found myself getting too nervous. And I already have enough to be stressed out about. I don't want to be stressed out about this pending alien invasion, too!

Past Life Regressionist #2: So, you just watched a life that has an awful future. But let's move through another life because we don't have too much time left. We can get though a couple more. So, let's just take a deep breath and relax and let go of any anxiety and ask for Source's light to come in from the top of your head, make its way down your body and release. And take another deep breath in. With the breath coming in, you feel yourself relaxing. And with the breath out, you feel yourself letting go of any tension, anxiety, stress, that you may be feeling.

Aliya: Okay. Better now.

Past Life Regressionist #2: Alright. So, let's... Let's open to a different life. A life that Noatok suggests that may be helpful for Aliya to gain a better understanding of who she is. Can you turn to a life like that, please?

Aliya: I'm hearing... Like, I see my book opening and I'm like running my hands across all the pages and I'm saying, all these make-up me. So, that would not be realistic (to see one life that would describe me).

Past Life Regressionist #2: Okay. Alright. Well, what about a life where Aliya stepped into her power as a Divine being?

Aliya: Okay. I think I'm getting the idea that there's a lot. I just have to pick one. I'm seeing one where there's a lady kind of holding up her arms (in a surrender). I don't... But that's what's coming through. It's not from a page though. It's just like... A lady with her arms up. Oh, wait. I think that's me now. Just a little older.

This image wasn't embedded on a particular page. It looked more like a six-inch hologram of myself, draped in a white gown, projecting over the pages of the book.

Past Life Regressionist #2: So, in this life. Okay.

Aliya: Yeah. Because it didn't show up on a page. It just like, this older lady, with their arms up. But I think it did show up on the page because it's just me now.

Past Life Regressionist #2: Alright. Well... Let me ask this. If you look around, do you see any Keepers around you or anyone there?

Aliya: My door is closed. But usually, he comes in when he knows I'm here and he sits with me. I think because I have a visitor and… Oh! This is neat. I see you sitting on the opposite side of the table.

Past Life Regressionist #2: Oh, that's cool.

Aliya: So, I have a visitor. And so, it's, like, I'm in, a little private… One of those library rooms.

I was sitting at the table where I usually sit. I was looking at the closed door, because that's where The Keeper would enter from, but then I scanned to the left and sitting in a chair across from me was the regressionist. This was the first time I'd seen a regressionist in a space with me. Retrospectively, I'm glad that I had the regressionist state the rules so that she could also enter this space with me.

Past Life Regressionist #2: Got it.

Aliya: So, he's not gonna come.

Past Life Regressionist #2: Okay. So, would you like to find some help to get you into one of these two lives? One that Noatok suggests or one of you as a Devine being?

Aliya: No. I get it.

Past Life Regressionist #2: Okay. This question is now to Aliya. Would you like to end the session here? We have a few more minutes. Do you want to go to your Higher Self because we didn't discuss that.

Aliya: *Um.* Yeah. We can try to call the Higher Self forward.

Past Life Regressionist #2: Okay. So, we are now going to leave this space. Allowing the entities from the past lives to recede back to a time and place where they belong. With much love and thanks for the help and information they've given us today. I would also like to allow any Spirit Guides or anyone else that has come forward in this space to recede back to the time and place where they belong. And now I would like for all the consciousness and personality of Aliya to return back to the body fully. May I please speak with Aliya's Higher Self?

Aliya: *Yes.*

Past Life Regressionist #2: May I... Do I have permission to ask the Higher Self questions?

Aliya: *Yes.*

Past Life Regressionist #2: Thank you. Though I understand that you could have shown us many different past lives today. But you chose to show us the lives that you did. Can you... Why did you show us those lives today?

Aliya: *Hmm. Those weren't lives that I showed you. Those were lives that Aliya asked for.*

Past Life Regressionist #2: Alright. Well. Out of the lives from the future, there was one that was picked from the book. Is there anything that you can do to help her with any anxieties she may feel from watching that life?

Alya: Just hearing, *"It's inevitable. You look and you will see."*

Past Life Regressionist #2: Is there any trauma or any energy from any of the past lives that would be helpful for us to clear today?

Aliya: *She carries a lot of trauma and pain and experiences with her. There's really nothing to clear. She does a good job at clearing and she's been doing it for a while. She just has to understand that somethings stick, because they make her, her. And everything doesn't need to be cleared even if it's a perceived deficient.*

Past Life Regressionist #2: And is there anything that the Higher Self would like to add? Add to any of the questions that were already answered today?

Aliya: *Um. Aliya had asked me (previously), the Higher Self, to be nicer and gentle and calmer and understanding. I am a reflection of how she treats herself. So, she's treating herself better. So, I'm showing up as better. But she has to extend the same grace to herself that she wants me to extend to her.*

Past Life Regressionist #2: Is that also why the Higher Self, sometimes in sessions with her client, comes in with a little bit of attitude or snarkiness? Is that related to the same concept?

Aliya: *Her Higher Self doesn't come in with sessions of the client. So, any snarkiness and dealing with Higher Self is from the client.*

Past Life Regressionist #2: Okay. Got it. Alright. Do you have any messages for humanity?

Aliya: I don't know why, my Higher Self laughed. Messages though? I'm just hearing, *"Buckle up."* Just like a, laugh and, *"Buckle up."*

Past Life Regressionist #2: Okay. And anything else other than what you mentioned about her treating herself a little bit nicer? Is there anything else that Aliya should be aware of that we haven't covered in the session?

Aliya: *No. She's getting through it. She's doing a lot of work on herself.* And so, what I'm feeling, is like, my Higher Self feels more lighter than before. And I'm getting the feeling that the more I work on myself, the easier it will be for me to have a connection with my Higher Self. And it won't be so hard. Like, it won't be like an extension of me, it will *be* me. So that's... That's the feeling I'm getting, is just advice to just keep working on myself, and as I do, I bring the Higher Self closer to me.

Past Life Regressionist #2: Good. Okay. And. *Um.* Aliya had some questions if we ran into some Keepers, any Keepers in the Akashic Records. Would it be okay if I asked you those questions instead?

Aliya: *Okay.*

Past Life Regressionist #2: So, what is her connection with The Keepers?

Aliya: *She knows them. She has a relationship with them. They love her. She works with them. They miss her while she's gone.*

Past Life Regressionist #2: Why is The Keeper helping counsel her?

Aliya: *She keeps showing up there.*

Past Life Regressionist #2: Okay.

Aliya: *And she's powerful. She keeps showing up because that feels like home to her. And she misses it a lot.* I'm getting emotional again. *But she misses it a lot. So, she's drawn there. And she goes there more times than she knows. Almost every night, she returns home, because she's desperate for…desperate for stability. And that's what she finds there. And they know and understand this. And they've tried to get her to stop coming.*

Past Life Regressionist #2: Okay.

Aliya: *But they realize that they can't stop her. And so, they sit and listen to her and offer advice as a parent would to a child.*

Past Life Regressionist #2: When you say she wants to go back home… Like, does she work at the Akashic Records?

Aliya: *Yes. It's where she spends her… She's deeply connected there, and she knows this, so I can explain it to you. But we don't have to explain it to her.*

Past Life Regressionist #2: Okay. Well, she was just asking what her roles and duties are there.

Aliya: *She was shown this before. I can explain it again, but she knows.*

Past Life Regressionist #2: Okay. Alright. And she knows why she was chosen for the job?

Aliya: *I think that was discussed.*

I actually don't know what my job is. On one occasion, when I'd asked The Keeper about my connection, he told me that I was a Superintendent in the Akashic Records. As with everything, when he told me that, I fully understood, although I was searching my brain to find the right human word because I knew the English definition and his definition of the word, "Superintendent", wasn't the same. And, I was only given the job title, not the roles or responsibilities.

Then, on a separate occasion, I presented myself to the regular library part of the Akashic Records (normally, I automatically show up in my golden room) and asked for The Keeper give me a tour of the Akashic Records and to explain what my role was there. The Keeper asked me if I was visiting as Aliya or Iman. I knew if I chose, Aliya, that the information he gave me would be limited to the human perspective (there would be limitations to my access to knowledge). So, I said, "Iman".

Immediately, I had on a robe, similar to his. My mind settled and felt still. I didn't have a real worry in the world. I knew everything I was supposed to know and none of it was concerning. We walked down a hallway, side-by-side. I didn't ask any questions, I knew where we were going. We got to a room and four other beings in cloaks surrounded me. We talked about my current life on Earth, and they told me that they missed me. We talked for a while, but I can't remember what was said and I don't remember leaving.

So, the question of, 'What the heck do I do at the Akashic Records?' still eludes me...

Past Life Regressionist #2: Okay. Alright. And does the Higher Self have any messages for me as we're gonna close up the session?

Aliya: I'm just getting the same. Like, the same, what Source said, that just, *you guys are on similar paths. So, any message for Aliya could be used for you, and vice versa.*

Past Life Regressionist #2: Alright. Wonderful. Well. Thank you very much for all the help and information that you've given us today. Our time here is at an end.

Aliya Griffin

Chapter Twenty-Three

In this final chapter, I want to revisit some important reflections. This book wasn't meant to serve as a complete guide on how or why Noatok connected with me and my clients. Instead, I set out to share a glimpse of his vibrant energy—as a way to gently lift the veil on our everyday perceptions of this incredible human experience journey. I hold a deep hope that as my path unfolds, even more stories of Noatok's radiant visits will come to light.

What's missing from the pages of this book, and what I don't know if I could ever do justice in describing, is the energy of the sessions when Noatok connected. The raw emotions of peace, love, joy, happiness and true harmony cannot be described using mere human descriptors. Whenever Noatok connected to myself and my clients, the energetic shift was felt immediately. Connecting to him was like the highest of highs that anyone could desire to reach. There was an air of divinity that could not be properly explained. There is a knowing and understanding that we are all connected by a force so much larger than ourselves, that ultimately makes us feel small in the vastness of infinity.

That connection was easily seen through each of the clients featured within these pages. I was specifically told during Clients A, B and C's sessions that I was connected to them. For Client A, our connection was her game, which I'm allowed to help her play, when and only when she reaches out to me first. For Clients B and C, our connection was described as something deeper. The connection to them felt more aligned to being soul tribe members. This conclusion seems confirmed, per Client C, we are connected beyond this life. Could that have been why Noatok decided to come through in their sessions and not the countless others that I'd done?

During my session with Past Life Regressionist #2, Noatok had suggested that he came through during client sessions because my own belief became stronger when another person witnessed the event. Yet, I can't help but feel there's more to the story. All four clients possessed incredibly powerful spiritual gifts, and I wonder if that shared sensitivity is what drew Noatok to connect with them. If you noted, Client's B, C and myself (through my own past life regression) connected to Noatok energetically through nature. Each of us found ourselves in a native community of some sort, connecting. Is that also our connection? Nature? Or is nature the source of Noatok's connection? Still, more answers.

Perhaps his visits were not just about validating my experiences and spiritual transformation, but also about meeting kindred spirits—fellow empaths whose hearts beat to a similar, profound rhythm. This seems plausible as his connection to Client's A, B and C were to benefit them on their individual human experience journey and Client D's session was the only client connection directly related to my journey. Although, I also need to mention that the mere presence of Noatok in my clients' sessions is reflective of his love, support and dedication to me.

What is Noatok?

Let's dig a little deeper into what Noatok's presence truly represents. According to Client C, he isn't just any empath—he's something altogether more potent, a "Heyoka empath." This term isn't tossed around lightly; A Heyoka empath's energy is far beyond the ordinary. Before we delve into what a Heyoka empath is, first, let's review what it means to be an empath.

Being an empath isn't simply about feeling emotions; it's like standing at the edge of a vast ocean, where each wave represents someone else's joy, sorrow, anxiety, or pain. I often experience these emotions as if they were my own, as vivid and immediate as the colors of a sunset splashed across the sky. This heightened sensitivity allows me to offer genuine compassion and healing to others, acting as a gentle guide through their inner landscapes. Yet, it's also a challenge—at times, the boundaries between my emotions and those of the people around me blur, creating a tapestry of feelings that can be both beautiful and overwhelming.

To be an empath is to see beyond the surface, to uncover the hidden truths woven into everyday moments. It's about helping others connect with their own feelings and to understand and embrace the full spectrum of their emotional lives. In this role, I become a bridge, linking hearts and souls with a quiet understanding that speaks louder than words. This is the essence of our shared human experience—a delicate dance of energy, emotion, and an ever-deepening connection to the universe.

A Heyoka empath is a rare and powerful type of empath known for their unconventional and transformative way of helping others. Rooted in the Native American Lakota and Dakota traditions, the word "heyoka" means "sacred clown" or "fool". As an empath, Noatok's playful energy can lighten even the heaviest situations, making healing feel less overwhelming and make painful truths easier to face. With Noatok's energy connected to mine, I feel a little less alone and as mentioned previously, less crazy. I'm not the only person witnessing his spiritual presence in my life or our divine connection. Through each of these clients, I'm provided tangible evidence of my and Noatok's energetic connection.

I first encountered Noatok's energy much like witnessing a sprite in full flight—a light, mischievous presence. In my initial session with Client A, my introduction to Noatok, his energy felt like that of a trickster: unexpected and vibrant. During that session, I remember confessing that "sprite" was the closest word I could muster to think of, even though it barely scratched the surface of what I felt. This is also why I believe Client C used the term Heyoka empath in her description for him, as that's the term her brain could come up with at the time. He is neither, but something far greater and indescribable. But since a Heyoka empath is the closest descriptor I have for a being such as him, we'll continue to use this terminology to unpack his energy.

Although Noatok presents as a cute, playful and mischievous child, Heyoka empaths are more than masters of playful mischief. Noatok serves as a spiritual mirror, reflecting back the hidden emotions, patterns, and behaviors I and my clients try to ignore. Noatok's very presence disrupts my usual way of thinking and challenges me to confront what I've long kept buried. For me, Noatok's presence has been nothing short of revolutionary, shaking up my understanding of both the physical and the spiritual realms.

Noatok appeared when my transformation was at a tipping point—I was wrapped in the throes of a spiritual awakening as my old beliefs and patterns were crumbling away. In the chaotic moments of my spiritual transformation, his energy acted like a cosmic reset button, nudging me to let go of what no longer served me so that I could embrace a new, more authentic reality. If you'll remember from earlier, part of my spiritual awakening was to embrace myself fully and authentically.

Before my awakening, I couldn't dream of announcing my spiritual gifts to the world. Even when everything pointed towards me living more authentically, I'd resisted. Funnily enough, it was Client C (during the psychic reading she'd performed on me months prior to our past life regression session) who told me that I could no longer hide who I was. Part of my transformation was releasing the fear I had surrounding letting people see my gifts and as a result, see me as I truly am, a psychic, medium/channel and empath. She urged me to embrace my true authentic self, letting me know that the outcome of doing such a thing would be better than I expected.

Noatok's presence was synchronistic to what Client C had told me. How could I hold tight to the idea that there was nothing special about me, if I had an energy as powerful as Noatok connected to me? It's as though Source gave him permission to reveal himself to me as a way to catapult me on my path, to speed up this transformation in an effort to specifically shake up the beliefs that used to guide my everyday thought process. As I shed old beliefs, relationships that no longer serve me, and old and disruptive patterns, I'm trying to embrace a new and unfamiliar reality, as well. Which is pretty damn hard.

This process is chaotic and disorienting. And is why Noatok showed up in my life when he did. Noatok is my Guide and a disruptor, helping me to break through illusions so that I can align with my Higher Self. He's also helping by breaking my ego attachments, highlighting misalignments and grounding me into this wonderful and magical experience that is life. I'm being challenged to work on my ego, release my pride, fears, and resistance to change.

Through Noatok, I have no choice but to reflect on what no longer serves me. I cannot go back to my old ways of thinking as that mundane world no longer exists for me. My connection to him brings a sense of groundedness and perspective.

Noatok's behavior may seem contradictory. He's both wise and childlike. I suspect that this duality allows him to connect deeply with myself and clients while defying expectations. Noatok, like Heyoka empaths, embody paradoxes that force others to let go of rigid thinking patterns and embrace the fluidity of life. Beyond their words or actions, Heyoka empaths often possess a powerful energetic presence that facilitates healing simply by being near.

After reading all of this, you may be asking yourself, why in the heck would I ever want my life disrupted like this? And you would be asking yourself that for a very good reason. Having this type of encounter is beautiful and spiritual, but as stated above, also disruptive, confusing, scary and lonely. While the Heyoka empath's methods may feel uncomfortable or even chaotic, the presence of a Heyoka empath is ultimately a profound gift. They bring clarity, transformation, and healing in ways that are as unique as they are effective. For someone navigating the heights of a spiritual awakening, the Heyoka empath's role is to act as a bridge between the old self and the awakened self, helping the person embrace their truth with courage and authenticity.

Their help is not always gentle, but it is always sacred. A Heyoka empath embodies the paradox of transformation: they break things apart to make them whole again, reminding us that true growth often begins in discomfort and ends in liberation. Noatok spoke of this during past life regressionists #1's session. He specifically spoke of building and setting things up for me in the background and asked me to trust and not interfere with his designs.

Soul/Spirit Baby

For Clients B and C, they'd recognized Noatok's energy as their son. Puzzling for sure, because why? Was it part of his "trickster" energy or had he presented as their son as a hint for me? A question to be asked during our next encounter. For Client C, Noatok told her he would be there to guide her back to her spiritual place in the forest. This alone would indicate that his connection to her is not dependent on me. But why and how if he's my soul baby? More questions that need answering.

In spiritual and metaphysical beliefs, the concept of a spirit baby is often thought of as a soul that exists in the spiritual realm, waiting to incarnate and join two souls as their child. In the context of this book, the term spirit baby means a baby that my soul has birthed. Because of this connection, Noatok and I have a shared energetic connection and as such, we're able to communicate through dreams and mediation and intuitive feelings. Ultimately, the idea of a spirit baby is a beautiful way of recognizing the deep spiritual connection that can exist between parents and their spirit child that is grounded in love, intention, and soul alignment.

Does Noatok have reincarnations?

After reading about Noatok, it would be logical to assume that his energy is too powerful for the constraints of a physical body. He's an enigma: a being of such magnitude and purity that even Source says he can't be contained by human form. However, despite that, we've witnessed him experiencing past lives. In Client B's past life, he was her son, John, without any spiritual gifts. And during my own past life regression, he was *my* son. A little boy so extraordinarily talented, that by the age of four, he was already bending reality with telekinesis, all because it had made him laugh. And in that life, I didn't see him grown because he'd left to travel through portals. Whew!

But here's something that makes this all even more magical: My theory suggests that the little boy that I see and am connected to, and the little boy that Clients B, C and D encountered is the same little boy from the past life I'd seen and shared with him in past life regressionist #2's session. This theory of mine adds a layer of humor to the situation, especially when you consider that each of us is working with a child—an energetic child who communicates telepathically because he doesn't share our language. Can you see the humor in that? A Brazilian little boy, although only four to six years old but wised beyond our human scope, attempting to communicate without the confines of words and without full insight into the complexities of the adult world that surrounds him.

Looking at it from that point of view makes me feel even that more special. Special that he'd heard me. Special that he's helping me. And I want to protect him. Protect this little precious boy who has incarnated to this earthly plane to experience the joys of being human, if only for a short while.

But this boy is not just playful, he's potent and yes, he's guiding me, helping me from behind the spiritual scenes while I, wrestling with my own human experiences, knock down his creations because of my limited beliefs and need for control. Although I don't want to get in his way, I know I have many times. As I desperately strive to move forward and keep pushing myself and thought processes further and further away from my traditional human beliefs, there's a small part of me that's reluctant to abandon my lifetime of human conditioning. I can only imagine that Noatok is frustrated with me because I don't understand his or my full potential.

Through all the challenges I've faced, there's one undeniable truth, Noatok has altered my life irrevocably. Through him, I'm learning to truly see myself and not just through human eyes, but through the eyes of the Soul. Noatok has shown me lessons that go beyond teaching. Through his connection, I'm forced to reckon with the material world less and embrace the energetic one more.

This is the magic of being a spirit parent, that energetic tie. My cry for help—a shift in consciousness—summoned him, and instead of giving me the answers I thought I'd wanted, he's giving me exactly what I need. Love. And that's where the lesson truly begins. Noatok is not here for me to "use" him, but rather, to teach me through my own growth, to support me through the transformation, and to help me navigate this spiritual awakening—no matter how painfully it unfolds.

My Spiritual Journey

Spiritual journeys, I believe, are meant to be challenging. We often picture awakenings as serene moments of bliss and clarity, yet in truth, they are among the most arduous and painful transformations we can experience. Awakening isn't merely about acquiring knowledge—it's a profound metamorphosis. It demands that we dismantle the old structures, beliefs, and identities that have long confined and defined us as human. Before mine, I hadn't thought about a spiritual journey or awakening. The only thing I knew about astrology were the sun signs and some minor characteristics of each. I'd never picked up a book about souls or spirituality. I can't name a spiritual deity to save my life. Kundalini? It's a word that I come across, but what the heck is that? In short, I didn't deal in the "woo woo" other than to play with tarot cards, leaning this far into it hadn't been on my 2024 Bingo card.

I'd seen a short video while writing this book. The host made the distinction between those who'd made a conscious decision to study spirituality as a way to transcend and awaken their souls and others who'd been pushed into it not by their own design. I am part of the latter group. Fresh from a divorce from a twenty-year marriage, kids all grown and living their own lives, me trying to figure out who I was, experiencing a life of freedom for the first time, hanging out and partying with new friends and lovers, then a trickle…a trickle of unhappiness, a trickle that there was something more. Then BOOM, I was thrust into the unknown, finding myself stumbling, trying to find my footing.

Picture standing at the edge of a familiar landscape built on life experiences so predictable that surprises aren't surprises, they're expectations. Suddenly, that familiar landscape crumbles beneath you, forcing you to step into an unknown terrain, compounding this fear is that you don't know if the ground before you, is solid and stable, or if it will swallow you whole. I know this imagery sounds overly dramatic, it's true. As I'm continuing to shed the layers of my identity that I've built over a lifetime, this transformation feels as if the ground I stood on was dissolving, leaving me feeling unsettled, unsafe, exposed and raw.

One of the most painful parts of the awakening/journey for me is the disintegration of my ego. I use the word, "is" because this is a long and arduous process that I'm still going through today. My ego, while it has come very far from where I began, still clings to familiar labels, roles, and societal expectations, always in search of control and certainty. But I know that to truly awaken, I have to surrender to the unknown—which feels like a death of the self, an identity crisis where I'm having a hard time recognizing who I now am – and who I once was.

An ego death means I would have to let go of who I *thought* I was. Try as hard as I might, like Source and Noatok said, I only get so far before I get scared and try to reach back for my old life. An ego death is just as the term states, it feels like I'm losing everything that I used to hold dear; my career, my livelihood, my friends, family, lovers, in essence, the life that I'd carefully curated for the past fifty years. Even though I can feel the abundance and freedom on this new path, I still get scared of advancing and leaving bits of myself behind.

But that's what I'm supposed to be going through and doing. I'm supposed to be wrestling with moving forward, working my way through this transformation, while having bouts of panic and doubts. I recall during past life regressionist #1's session, Source revealed that my old ways were being unraveled. It hurts, profoundly so, as familiar patterns are being dismantled, and new ones are taking shape. To truly awaken, I realize I have to dismantle everything I thought I knew about being human— every piece, every belief. That means daring to go against the grain of society.

As Source said, this is a process that I have to work through myself. The hidden corners of my being are being illuminated— the deep-seated fears, old wounds, and the conditionings I've tried so hard to bury. These suppressed emotions often surge back in overwhelming waves, demanding that I confront the pain I've long avoided. This challenging process, often called "shadow work," is not for the faint of heart. It requires intense self-reflection, radical acceptance, and persistent healing. Yet, it is only by embracing and integrating these darker aspects of myself that I can truly illuminate the dark.

This spiritual journey has turned my entire world upside down. Suddenly, my relationships shifted, the career that I'd spent almost two decades building was no more, and the lifestyle that I'd secured by two Master's degrees and two post-graduate certificates was slipping through my fingers. The safe havens I'd built started to feel foreign, leaving me with a deep sense of isolation and loss. Superficial friendships quietly faded, family dynamics twisted, changed, righted, and the ambitions that once fueled my days no longer carried meaning.

All of this was sudden. It felt like the rug was pulled right from under my very feet. This stage—often called the "dark night of the soul"—felt like I wandered through a vast, shadowy forest, where uncertainty reigned, and every step forward required me to trust in something unseen.

My awakening demands that I surrender, that I let go of the illusion of control and instead lean into a higher intelligence beyond my immediate understanding. For someone like me, who is used to having all the answers, this leap of faith is downright terrifying. So, of course, my mind would naturally resist the idea of an open-ended journey without a clear map, but this spiritual growth is gently insisting that I release my need to figure it all out and instead allow life's mystery to guide me.

Through my awakening, my perceptions are shifting, much like the changing colors of a sunset. I'm now seeing the world through a new lens—one that often makes me feel out of place as those around me remain anchored in old ways of thinking. The fear of judgment or rejection can be a heavy burden, making it tempting to hide this transformation. Yet, I understand that part of my awakening is about standing in my own truth, even if it means I have to walk this lonely path. My journey is one of becoming, where the discomfort of letting go ultimately clears the way for a deeper, more authentic connection with the universe.

Again, I push forward, aware that this spiritual awakening, while excruciating, offers me a freedom like no other. My discomfort is the unmistakable sign that my old illusions are falling away, making space for my true self to emerge. Imagine watching a well-worn painting gradually fade away, revealing the raw, unfiltered canvas underneath. In this process, long-buried wounds and forgotten shadows resurface. These aren't just memories or regrets; they're vivid, pulsing reminders that parts of me have been hidden away, waiting for the light to be set free.

As someone who has been in therapy for years, working on my triggers and illuminating my shadows, this part of the transformation created stress. The childhood traumas that I'd thought were cleared were suddenly back. Fear of rejection, fear of abandonment and the scarcity mindset were not only back, but front and center. But this time, instead of glossing over those feelings, I was forced to peel back the layers of those painful feelings until I reached the center. The very reason for the raw emotion. I then gave myself permission to feel the way I felt, which in doing that—confronting the true cause, I was finally able to untangle my ego from those traumas and begin to release the old narrative that those feelings were attached to. This of course, continues to be an ongoing therapeutic process.

I often think of myself as a snake shedding its skin—each layer that peels away is a step closer to growth and renewal. This pain that I'm going through isn't a punishment; it's the work of being reborn. This journey isn't about becoming someone entirely new—it's about peeling away the conditioning to reveal to the world who I am at my core. It's like returning home to a long-forgotten part of my Soul, a place of authenticity and truth. Though the path may be rough and full of uncertainty, it remains the most beautiful road that I've ever traveled.

Walking this path is like traversing a tightrope where every step demands careful thought, and every word is chosen with intention. The journey is profoundly lonely because it's a personal battle to untangle the deep-seated thoughts and beliefs that used to define me. If I had a partner in this journey, I'd likely find myself so absorbed in helping them that I'd neglect my own growth. This is why, in the end, the focus must be on me—or on you, if you find yourself on this very path.

Waking up is undeniably hard. Even when my energy dips and the weight of the transformation feels overwhelming, I remind myself that I'm doing just fine. Each challenge is a step toward a more authentic, liberated self, and that makes every struggle worthwhile. I'm exactly where I need to be.

I keep moving forward because, again, I know what awaits me at the end of this journey: true freedom and awakening. I'm ready to embrace whatever comes my way, to stand in my truth and let the world see me as I am, bathed in the brilliant light of authenticity.

Final Thoughts

What a ride it's been! Writing this book wasn't a grueling task—it flowed naturally from a place of deep love. My hope in sharing even a glimpse of my spiritual journey is that it sparks something within you, encouraging you to explore your own path and discover that you are more than just your physical form, that there's a vast, unseen reality waiting to be experienced.

My adventure with Noatok is far from finished. I welcome his presence wholeheartedly—both in the visible and unseen realms. I cherish his gifts, his guidance, and the companionship he offers. I am immensely grateful to Source for allowing me to connect with such a radiant being of love and light.

As I close, I'm drawn to the image of a sunset—a symbol of transition, completion, and renewal. Noatok, in his mysterious way, chose his miracle to show me a sunset. Across cultures and beliefs, sunsets remind us of the natural cycles of life: the beauty in endings and the promise of fresh beginnings. They invite us to release what no longer serves us, making space for new insights and opportunities.

Sunsets represent the culmination of efforts and the completion of a cycle. Spiritually, it's a time to acknowledge our day's work, celebrating our accomplishments while also understanding that endings are a natural and necessary part of growth. As the day winds down, sunsets encourage quiet introspection. The serene beauty of the setting sun offers a moment to pause, reflect on the day's events, and find peace within ourselves.

A sunset signals that night will eventually give way to dawn, symbolizing the promise of renewal and new beginnings. It's a reminder that life is cyclical and that every ending is a prelude to something new. Sunsets are a liminal space between day and night, representing the harmony between light and shadow, the known and unknown. This balance teaches us to embrace duality and recognize the beauty in both highs and lows, light and darkness.

Watching the day come to a close can be a time to appreciate the blessings in our lives and the beauty around us, fostering a sense of gratitude for each day's experiences. Connection to the Divine and the Infinite: For many, a sunset is a deeply spiritual experience, connecting them to something greater. Its beauty and vastness can evoke feelings of oneness with the universe and the eternal, reminding us of our place in the grand design of life. Spiritually, the sunset is a reminder that each day is a gift, a journey, and an opportunity for reflection, appreciation, and growth. It symbolizes the delicate balance of life and the potential for transformation with every cycle.

Noatok has forever changed my life. Through him, I've learned to see myself in new transformative ways. His presence, through embodying the innocence of a child, is powerful and deeply loving—a connection born from my own cry for help and an undeniable energetic pull. My spiritual awakening has been as painful as it has been eye-opening. I'm breaking free from the confines of a limited human experience, my eyes gradually adjusting to the magic of this world and those beyond. Although this journey is often lonely, the knowledge that I am not alone serves as a lifeline—a rope thrown to me as I struggle to stay afloat amid the stormy seas. And as Noatok reminds me, he's offering me the support I need, not the help I think I want. I'm learning that his role is to guide me as I step further into my own awakening.

Source has done its part in letting Noatok through to help me. Now, it's up to me to trust and have faith in the process. And most importantly, not to stress out this little boy from a different time and space who's just trying to help his mom move through a powerful spiritual transformation.

Noatok showed up to reveal me, *to me*. Through him I was able to finally see me. I know that I'm the connection in all of this and because of that I must be special. His presence reminds me of who I am and of my soul's purpose. I'm human, living out this human experience and of course I face doubt. Sometimes I believe and sometimes I don't, and that's ok. I'm able to pull myself out of low-vibrational energy, because that's what doubt is, low vibrational energy. And I can pull myself out by thinking of Noatok and how he's real to people besides myself and because of that, he's not a figment of *all* of our imaginations.

And through that recounting I can remember that he's here with me, guiding and helping. So, who I am and what I'm going through must be real. I've said twice before and I'll say it again, waking up is so darn hard. I must untangle from the human teachings and lies that are meant to keep us manageable. I realized along the way, that if I wake fully, I can lead others to wake up as well. So, I persist. Because while waking up is hard, it's also pretty damn exciting and wonderful.

Aliya Griffin

an open letter to aliya

one's real life is almost always the life one doesn't lead*   what we should do and what we do seldom coincide   i'm so proud of you for embracing the challenge to step out of the box and live your authentic 'self'   ...for being attentive to your higher self i've seen what happens to people when they stuff their real feelings down deep so they don't have to deal with them   they get sick and develop all sorts of illnesses   it's kinda scary to step out of 'the sheep-formation of simon says' and follow the beat of your own drum   ...your own path   recalibrating and renegotiating your recognition of 'self' and all that that embodies unrestricted by societal norms   ...your gifts are tools, and like any tool, in order for them to be effective, you have to use them but you've always been your own super hero   your own labor-intensive positive efforts and validation   ...you've always had a great insight for what you wanted   always know, your spirit has the energy to create the things you want and that your spirit guides are always with you in every step you take, watching you go through your decisions   ...watching you facing your own power

all we know is what's happening in consciousness

our deeds still travel with us from afar   and what we have been makes us what we are*

i'm excited for you, for what that path looks like and what it holds in store for you   my heart tells me, the journey is going to be even more wonderful than you can even imagine   you're bound for amazing adventures   i'm geeked to see what time reveals   this spiritual undertaking is just a prelude to an unimaginably beautiful journey   …so pump-up the volume and dance (after all, we are spiritual beings having human experiences not the other way around right)   …i'm glad you found your door

Diana Wimbish
(My mommy)

Practitioner Contacts

Aliya Griffin (Psychic, Past Life Regressionist) – Spiritual Girlie: www.spiritualgirlie.com

Nathaniel (Spiritual Mentor) – KayNa Spirit Centre: https://kaynaspiritcentre.com

Senate Notrem (Psychic) – Indulged Wellbeing: https://senatenotrem.com

Lies (Past Life Regressionist #1) – vanderveken_lies@hotmail.com

Sara (Past Life Regressionist #1) – https://hypnosisbeyond.com/

Aliya Griffin

About Aliya Griffin

Aliya Griffin is a psychic, medium/channel and empath. When she's not meeting with clients through her spiritual practice, she's writing books about her spiritual journey or she's writing romance books (via her pen name A.M. Griffin: www.amgriffnbooks.com). She is a believer in the unbelievable, open to all possibilities from mermaids in our oceans and seas, angels in the skies and intelligent life forms in distant galaxies.

I love hearing from my readers. Like one of my books? Drop me a line! thespiritualgirlie@gmail.com

Visit www.spiritualgirlie.com to find out more about Aliya Griffin.

Stay in touch!

Aliya Griffin

this little light of mine – an ald negro spiritual – written by harry dixon loes in the 1920's

one's real life is almost always the life one doesn't lead – anonymous

our deeds still travel with us from afar   and what we have been. makes us what we are – george eliot